$35.00
12/08/2011

J
974.71
R

ROOSEVELT PUBLIC LIB

The Empire State Buildin

36649001627050

D1305495

BUILDING AMERICA
THEN AND NOW

THE
EMPIRE STATE BUILDING

BUILDING AMERICA: THEN AND NOW

BUILDING AMERICA
THEN AND NOW

THE
EMPIRE STATE BUILDING

RONALD A. REIS

CHELSEA HOUSE
PUBLISHERS
An imprint of Infobase Publishing

The Empire State Building

Copyright © 2009 by Infobase Publishing

All rights reserved. No part of this book may be reproduced or utilized in any form or by any means, electronic or mechanical, including photocopying, recording, or by any information storage or retrieval systems, without permission in writing from the publisher. For information contact:

Chelsea House
An imprint of Infobase Publishing
132 West 31st Street
New York, NY 10001

Library of Congress Cataloging-in-Publication Data
Reis, Ronald A.
   The Empire State Building / by Ronald A. Reis.
      p. cm. — (Building America)
   Includes bibliographical references and index.
   ISBN 978-1-60413-045-4 (hardcover)
   1. Empire State Building (New York, N.Y.)—Juvenile literature. 2. New York (N.Y.)—Buildings, structures, etc.—Juvenile literature. I. Title. II. Series.
   F128.8.E46R45 2009
   974.7'1—dc22   2008025549

Chelsea House books are available at special discounts when purchased in bulk quantities for businesses, associations, institutions, or sales promotions. Please call our Special Sales Department in New York at (212) 967-8800 or (800) 322-8755.

You can find Chelsea House on the World Wide Web at http://www.chelseahouse.com

Text design by Annie O'Donnell
Cover design by Ben Peterson

Printed in the United States

Bang FOF 10 9 8 7 6 5 4 3 2 1

This book is printed on acid-free paper.

All links and Web addresses were checked and verified to be correct at the time of publication. Because of the dynamic nature of the Web, some addresses and links may have changed since publication and may no longer be valid.

CONTENTS

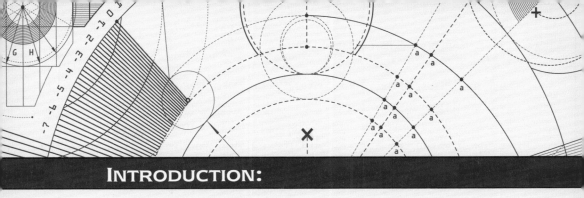

A New Day Dawning

At first, they just swiped stuff—specifically the embroidered towels. After all, what guest would not want a keepsake from what was, in the 1920s, arguably the nation's (if not the world's) finest hotel? Next, the souvenir seekers took pen to paper, over a thousand of them, and wrote to the Waldorf-Astoria's management, asking for all manner of goodies, some still bolted down to the 12–16-story structure. The hotel, which had closed in spring 1929, was now, in late September, marked for demolition. Everyone wanted a piece of what was not already auctioned off or sold outright by the new owners of the choice midtown New York site at Fifth Avenue and 34th Street.

A man from Keokuk, Iowa, wrote asking for the iron fence that ran the length of the building on Fifth Avenue. A woman in Connecticut wanted a balcony railing for her country house. A man in Maine requested a flagpole. Someone in Miller River, Washington, made an appeal for the hotel's famous stained-glass windows. One man and his wife were, as declared in *Building the Empire State Building*, "made very happy by being able to secure the key to the room they had occupied many years before while on their honeymoon."

Not all was given up, sold, or scrapped. The mural paintings were salvaged, as was some of the interior woodwork. They would continue life in the new, modern Waldorf-Astoria being constructed on the fashionable corner of Lexington Avenue and 49th Street.

A century earlier, the plot that would eventually hold the Waldorf-Astoria Hotel was farmland, located uptown and four miles from the commercial development at Manhattan's southern tip. By the 1850s, however, large mansions were being built in the area, two of which were owned by members of the elite Astor family. In 1890, William Waldorf Astor inherited his father's house on 33rd Street and Fifth Avenue. His neighbor and aunt, Caroline Astor, acquired the adjoining house and property that fronted 34th Street.

The two Astors despised each other, and one was always looking for a way to upstage the other. To spite his aunt (and to take advantage of the rising demand for commercial property in the area), William—who moved out of his home in 1890—schemed to construct a hotel in its place tall enough to cast a disagreeable shadow over Caroline's property. The result was the erection of the 12-story Waldorf in 1893.

Aunt Caroline, who was annoyed, countered by abandoning her home, moving farther uptown, and then having an even grander, 16-story hotel (the Astoria) built on the site in 1897.

Rather than continue battling, however, the two Astors reluctantly agreed to a truce—it was better to make money than to fight! William and Caroline joined their two hotels to form the opulent, exclusive, world-class Waldorf-Astoria Hotel.

The new hotel boasted a 1,500-seat grand ballroom. It had 1,000 rooms and featured "room service," which enabled guests to have breakfast in bed. Also included was a long corridor through which ladies could parade, displaying their gowns, jewels, and gaudy plumage. The strutting promenade became known as "Peacock Alley."

Nonetheless, as America moved into the modern, fast-paced, post-World War I age, styles and tastes quickly changed. By the late 1920s, the Waldorf-Astoria Hotel had become decidedly out of date and, just as important, out of place.

With midtown Manhattan (particularly along Fifth Avenue between 23rd and 59th streets) becoming a more upscale, first-class retail subdivision (featuring the likes of Tiffany & Co.), owners of the hotel decided to sell their valuable holding, let the

The Waldorf and Astoria Hotels stood on the future site of the Empire State Building. The hotels had become a symbol of glamour and luxury in America. A grand marble promenade connecting the two buildings, known as Peacock Alley *(above)*, became so famous it drew an estimated 25,000 visitors every day.

buyers do what they would with the property, and rebuild their Waldorf-Astoria in a new part of town. When the Bethlehem Engineering Corporation bought the two-acre site in December 1928, the $13,500,000 (roughly $173.5 million in 2008 values) it paid became the highest price ever for a piece of land in New York City. Within months, however, the Bethlehem deal fell apart. The company failed to make the second of two cash installments of $2,500,000 (about $32 million today). The property again came on the market.

Whoever was to buy the Waldorf-Astoria would have to do something spectacular with the site, because the land had cost so much. Furthermore, tearing down the antiquated hotel would be a high-cost undertaking in itself. What could take its place that would justify the huge investment in land and building necessary to turn a profit? It would have to be an edifice that was truly glorious and inspiring yet practical and moneymaking.

When the new buyers (who formed the Empire State Group) announced their ambitions, *Fortune* magazine declared, "If the owners are right, they may fix the center of the Metropolis. If they are wrong, they will have the hooting of the experts in their ears for the rest of their lives."

What would come to pass would be a structure unlike any other. The Empire State Building was to be the largest and tallest skyscraper in the world. Initial plans called for an art deco masterwork to rise a thousand feet and include 80 stories of rental space. The high-rise would completely fill the 84,000-square-foot site of the Waldorf-Astoria. It would, the builders hoped, accelerate midtown's stride toward commercial prominence and pull more business uptown. The Empire State's construction and tenancy, its visionaries declared, would see a new day dawning—for New York, for America, and for the world.

CHAPTER 1

Birth of the Skyscraper

The Exposition Universelle, or World's Fair of 1889, would need something spectacular to set it off and attract millions of visitors, all to celebrate the one-hundredth anniversary of the French Revolution. Gustave Eiffel had demonstrated a talent for building with iron and steel, having supervised the construction of numerous metal bridges and viaducts throughout Europe in the mid-nineteenth century. In 1885, the brilliant mechanical engineer had been called upon to design the metal framework for France's gift to America, the Statue of Liberty. Still, could he come through for the French fair? Eiffel's tower plans for the 1888 Barcelona Universal Exposition had been rejected. Would France now take a chance on him?

Yes, it would. The result, though designed to be temporary and torn down at the fair's end, is still there today for countless individuals to admire and ascend. The engineer's Eiffel Tower was built 986 feet tall and included 18,038 pieces of puddled iron joined with over two-and-a-half million rivets; it was, and still is, a technological wonder of the industrial age. Upon completion, the tower was also a portent of building construction methods and materials that would dominate in the next century.

Tall structures, of course, had been around forever. Two of the original Seven Wonders of the Ancient World—the Mausoleum at Halicarnassus and the Temple of Artemis at Ephesus—were quite tall, the former standing 140 feet high. The medieval cathedrals of Europe truly reached for the sky—all the better to please the heavens. Yet such temples and churches, constructed for the most part of stone and concrete, were never intended to provide living or working space in their higher reaches. As tall as steeples and campaniles were, they barely had room for a single ladder to be climbed by a lone keeper.

The problem in such buildings lay in their stone and brick construction. The entire structure was supported by its walls; thus, as the tower grew in height, the walls bore more load. Such load-bearing walls had to be extremely thick at their base, though they thinned out somewhat as they rose. Still, for tall structures, the walls remained too thick to allow for rooms with any measurable floor space.

The same problem extended to apartments, offices, and factory lofts in the industrial cities of the eighteenth and nineteenth centuries. The brick and stone walls carried the floor beams as the building grew taller. Not only did the lower walls require a thick base, but the space for windows was limited as well; too big a gap would weaken the wall. Bearing-wall construction had height limits that usually extended no more than six stories.

In 1883, the Home Insurance Company of Chicago asked William Le Baron Jenney, an engineering and architecture graduate of Paris's École Centrale des Arts et Manufactures, to design an office building for them. They wanted it to be 10 stories tall. Such a building—using traditional bearing-wall, masonry construction methods—would require fortresslike walls. A new approach was required.

Standing tall at 986 feet, the Eiffel Tower *(above)* in Paris is one of the most popular tourist attractions in the world and has received over 167 million visitors. In addition to the materials used to build the tower, 20,000 light bulbs are needed to illuminate the structure for special occasions and events.

One day, frustrated by his attempt to come up with a radical design solution, Jenney decided to head home from his office early. According to historian George Douglas, as quoted in Neal Bascomb's book *Higher: A Historic Race to the Sky and the Making of a City:*

> Jenney's wife was startled to see him so early and thought he might be ill. Getting up suddenly from her chair where she was reading, she looked around for the most handy place to set down her book, and accordingly laid it on top of a bird cage. . . .

FROM IRON TO STEEL

Iron and steel may look alike to the untrained eye, but there are big differences between the two. It is when iron and steel are put to use that the distinctions are most obvious. As Alfred Morgan, writing in *The Story of Skyscrapers*, illustrates, "Whitewash and milk may look somewhat alike but a big difference shows when they are used. Try to make pancakes with whitewash or paint the cellar with milk and see. There is the same similarity in appearance between iron and steel as there is between whitewash and milk and just as great a difference in their purpose."

Iron is found in rocks and earth. However, it is never found in its native state. One cannot mine iron as with gold, silver, or copper. Iron is always found in combination with other elements from which it must be extracted. Metallic iron is withdrawn from iron ore using coke and limestone in a blast furnace. This process is known as *smelting*.

Iron contains an excessive amount of carbon and other impurities. Steel is created by burning out most of the carbon and impurities from iron. Finished steel contains about one percent carbon. As a result, steel combines the flexibility of wrought iron (which has very little carbon) with the brute strength of cast iron (which has a great deal of carbon). Early steel was about 20 percent stronger than either wrought or cast iron. Today's steel is at least six times stronger than either.

Iron is changed into structural steel by burning out most of the impurities in an open-hearth furnace. Molten cast iron is poured into white-hot furnaces at the steel plant. When purified, the molten steel is first poured into a ladle and then into molds where, when cooled, it forms *ingots*, or huge blocks of metal. As Morgan notes, "This is just the same process as pouring water into molds to be set in a refrigerator and cooled into blocks of ice. The only difference is that the 'freezing' or solidifying point of liquid steel is way above that of water."

From this point, the steel is reheated in a "soaking pit" and then sent to the blooming mill, where the hot steel is shaped into rails, plates, shafts, and, of course, beams for building skyscrapers and bridges.

Jenney jumped with surprise when he noticed that this light-weight bird cage could support a heavy load without the slightest difficulty. Back to the office Jenney went with the clue to the skyscraper—"cage design."

The Home Insurance Building of Chicago, built in 1885, used metal cage framing on its upper stories; today it is considered America's, and thus the world's, first skyscraper—the foundation of a building revolution.

MOHAWK SKY BOYS

Caughnawaga is home to the Mohawk Indians in Quebec, Canada, not far from Montreal. By the time Europeans arrived in the sixteenth century, the Mohawks had been hunters in the region for ages. Around 1700, many became canoemen, freighting furs down the St. Lawrence River for the French. When the fur trade dried up in the 1850s, more than a few Mohawk men found themselves out of work. According to Joseph Mitchell, a *New Yorker* writer in the 1930s, "A good many became depressed and shiftless; these hung out in Montreal and did odd jobs and drank cheap brandy."

In 1886, all of that changed. The Dominion Bridge Company (DBC) of Canada leased reservation land and began to construct a huge, cantilevered metal railroad bridge across the St. Lawrence River just below a Caughnawaga village. As part of the deal to obtain land rights, the company promised to employ Caughnawagas whenever possible.

At first, the Mohawks became ordinary day laborers and mostly unloaded materials; however, that was not good enough for them. According to a DBC official, as quoted by Mitchell in the *New Yorker:*

They were dissatisfied with this arrangement and would come out on the bridge itself every chance they got. It was quite impossible to keep them off. As the work progressed, it became apparent to all concerned that these Indians were very odd in that they did not have any fear of heights. If not watched, they would climb up into the spans and walk around there as cool and collected as the toughest of our riveters, most of whom at that period were old sailing-ship men especially picked for their experience in working aloft. These Indians were as agile as goats.

Soon enough, the Mohawks became bridge builders. "It turned out that putting riveting tools in their hands was like putting ham with eggs," the DBC official declared. "In other words, they were natural-born bridgemen."

For a generation, all went well. Then, in 1907, everything imploded in a tragedy that is remembered and honored to this day. On the morning of August 29, during the erection of the Quebec Bridge across the St. Lawrence River, a loud grinding sound screeched forth. The span, which had been threatening to crack for days, collapsed and killed 96 men, 35 of whom were Caughnawagas.

Instead of depressing the Mohawks, however, the disaster made "high steel" all the more attractive, especially to young boys. They all wanted to work as bridge builders as a matter of pride.

If there were not enough bridges to build, the Mohawks would go wherever high steel work would take them. "A few gangs would go to this bridge and a few would go to that," declared Mitchell. "Pretty soon, there weren't enough bridge jobs, and the gangs began working on all types of high steel—factories, office buildings, department stores, hospitals, hotels, apartment houses . . . anything and everything."

In quick order, Canada got too small for the Caughnawagas—they started crossing the border. It was not long before the "Mohawk Sky Boys" descended on New York, which, at the turn of the twentieth century, was poised to become the "skyscraper city."

DOWNTOWN/UPTOWN

Within a few decades of the Republic's birth in 1776, Manhattan had become a flourishing commercial center. The

22.96-square-mile island boasted approximately 16 miles of shoreline, all the better to provide ample docking opportunities for sea traders. To be sure, business activity was concentrated at Manhattan's lower tip, where ships first encountered the island. It was here that a downtown metropolis would germinate and thrive.

In 1811, city planners took an economically far-reaching step when they divided Manhattan (except for its southern end below 14th Street) into a massive street grid. Avenues would run north and south; streets, east and west. Based on the assumption that commerce would concentrate on the long shorelines running up the Hudson and East rivers, many more streets were created than avenues, thus allowing for the anticipated crosstown transportation of goods from east to west.

Unfortunately, the city planners got it wrong. By the time of the Civil War (1861–1865), it was clear that the ebb and flow of New York traffic moved mostly on a north-south axis. As a result, getting uptown—to Washington Square and beyond—was becoming a nightmare. According to John Tauranac, in his book *The Empire State Building: The Making of a Landmark:*

> The streets were often riotous affairs, with horse-drawn delivery wagons and omnibuses fighting each other over turf, with the problem becoming so exacerbated by the beginning of the twentieth century that the city experienced nascent forms of gridlock. There were simply not enough avenues to handle the traffic, nor were they wide enough.

As commercial activity exploded, so did land values in the downtown area. It quickly became apparent to concentrate commercial enterprise, office buildings, and loft manufacturing at the south end of the island and let workers commute uptown to live in houses and apartments. To make a city of 3.5 million residents a fact, the New York Rapid Transit System was born; at first it consisted of elevated trains along the major avenues, and then, beginning in 1904, subways began to run beneath the thoroughfares.

With every square foot of land in lower Manhattan becoming more and more valuable, it was obvious that—if technology would allow it—erecting an office building taller would make a great deal of financial sense. It would take two developments,

BUILDING AMERICA NOW

LIBERTY PLACE

Location Philadelphia
Architect Murphy & Jahn
Height 945 ft. and 847 ft.
Materials Steel, Aluminum, and Glass
Completion Date 1987 and 1990

Located in downtown Philadelphia, the two Liberty Place towers are the tallest buildings not only in the city but also in the entire state of Pennsylvania. The towers, which consist of mixed-use office, shopping, and hotel space, are not identical—the first tower is 98 feet taller than the second and, according to some, a bit more elegant.

Inspired by the art deco of the 1920s and 1930s (in particular, New York's Chrysler Building), architect Helmut Jahn sought to recall the famous 1929 building with the terminal spar and pinnacle at the top of the first tower. Both towers have a steel structure that is formed by a central core containing elevators and eight large pillars around the perimeter. The interior is remarkably free of obstruction, leaving a maximum square footage for office space. Externally, the lower levels are lined with stone, while the rest of the two buildings are "skinned" with aluminum and glass panels. Chrysler Building architect William Van Alen would have been pleased.

however, for skyscrapers (buildings at least 20 stories high) to become a reality. There would have to be a way to forgo stair climbing beyond four or five floors, and a structural material would need to exist that could keep a tall building from blowing over in the wind. By the late nineteenth century, solutions to both challenges were at hand, in the form of elevators and steel beams.

Elisha Graves Otis did not invent the elevator. He created something even more significant: the elevator safety brake. In 1854, Otis took his newly constructed device to the Crystal Palace Exposition in New York. As a huge crowd looked on, the inventor ascended an open-sided platform high into the palace's airy enclosure. Then Otis stopped, looked around, and—with a dramatic sweep of his hand—instructed his assistant to cut the supporting rope using an axe. With a toothed guiderail located on each side to grab the free-falling platform, the hoist held fast. As a result, the elevator industry took off within the next few years, making it possible to surmount a building's step-climbing height limit.

"Americans," according to Jim Rasenberger, author of *High Steel: The Daring Men Who Built the World's Greatest Skyline*, "did not invent steel, but steel, in many ways, invented twentieth-century America." Six times as strong as iron, steel provided the strength to go tall. Thanks to Jenney's birdcage frame design, the structural integrity to brace against natural forces was at hand. Furthermore, a steel-framed building, as Rasenberger declared:

> turned the old rules of architecture inside out: instead of resting their weight on thick external walls of brick or stone, they placed it on an internal framework—a "skeleton"—of steel columns and beams. The effect was as if buildings had evolved overnight from lumbering crustaceans into lofty vertebrates. Walls would still be necessary for weather protection and adornment, but structurally they'd be almost incidental.

Thus, the economics and the technology for the skyscraper had materialized. Throw in a good dose of ego, and there was no telling how high developers were willing to go.

CATHEDRAL OF COMMERCE

Elevators and steel-frame construction combined allowed for ever-higher structures, with buildings that hung walls over their frames like curtains. Indeed, such walls would forever be referred to as *curtain walls*—walls that would eventually become nothing more than glass sheets.

The skyscraper could be thought of in human body form. Tauranac expressed it brilliantly when he declared:

> Your body is supported by a skeleton of bone, with muscle and cartilage holding it together. Your skin does not support the weight of your body; it simply hangs there. When your skin is pricked, you leak blood but you do not fall down. The average skyscraper is likewise supported by a skeleton of steel. Its skin, or walls, are supported by the frame; they do not support the building. When the wall of a skyscraper is pricked, it leaks air, and unless its skeleton has suffered a seriously deleterious blow, the building does not fall down.

Not everyone, however, was convinced that tall, steel-framed buildings would stay up. Many feared that, with a strong wind, a skyscraper would blow over.

In 1888, architect Bradford Gilbert was commissioned to design a building on a tiny plot of land on lower Broadway. The site was only 21 by 39 feet. Borrowing Jenney's birdcage design, Gilbert planned to stand a steel bridge structure on end. Eventually, after wearing down the critics who sought to discredit him, Gilbert was granted a permit for an 11-story structure, to be known as the Tower Building.

As the building rose, the proprietor next door put his property up for sale and left, fearing that—at the first strong wind—the structure would collapse. Then, according to Bascomb, "When construction neared completion, the Weather Bureau warned of hurricane gales on their way to hit the city. Gawkers crowded Broadway on Sunday morning to watch the building tumble. After all, many had read and seen photographs of bridges buckling and crumbling apart in such storms."

As the 80-mile-an-hour winds blew, Gilbert was to have said, as quoted by Bascomb, "I secured a plumb-line and began to climb the ladders that the workmen had left in place when they quit work the previous evening. . . . When I reached the [top] story, the gale was so fierce I could not stand upright. I crawled on my hands and knees along the scaffolding and dropped the plumb-line. There was not the slightest vibration. The building stood as steady as a rock in the sea."

The skyscraper had arrived, and its future was now assured.

A year after Gilbert's Tower Building went up, the 18-story World Building was built. In 1902, the still-standing, iconic, 21-story Flatiron Building rose up, so named because it resembled an iron used for pressing clothes. The 1908 Singer Building, 612 feet and 47 stories high, took the lead and seemed destined to hold it for eternity. The very next year, however, the Metropolitan Life Building shot skyward. It rose an incredible 700 feet.

Then, in 1913, the Woolworth Building was erected. Frank Woolworth, who had made his fortune selling trinkets for nickels and dimes in hundreds of Woolworth stores throughout the United States, was determined to build an office structure that would make money not only by renting space to tenants but also by advertising his name and business. To do so, the building would have to be the tallest in the world. Once identified as such, Woolworth was sure that fact alone would create a marketing bonanza.

The finished neo-Gothic-style, 59-story, 791-foot building remained the tallest anywhere until 1930. The $15 million office complex was fully rented the day it opened, when it was dubbed

Originally called the Fuller Building, New York's newest structure was soon renamed the Flatiron Building *(above)* for its resemblance to a laundry iron. Located on a notoriously windy corner, the tower is reinforced with a steel frame and covered with a façade of terra cotta and limestone. It is New York's oldest skyscraper.

the "Cathedral of Commerce." Woolworth had been right—and the era of skyscrapers as ego expression had begun.

DOWNTOWN'S DARK CANYONS

As skyscrapers rose hundreds of feet, one against the other, canyons appeared that were created, as Tauranac put it, "not by erosion but by economics." At street level, sunlight barely penetrated. Air—what there was of it—was stifling. Downtown New York had become, in the first decade of the twentieth century, a dark, foreboding place in which few wished to work or live.

Money, derived from rentable space, drove the desire to build not just tall but in bulk. Construction of the Equitable Building in 1916 forcefully reflected such lust and excess. According to Daniel Okrent, in *Great Fortune: The Epic of Rockefeller Center:*

> The Equitable Building was a far more efficient—if less glamorous—economic machine than the Woolworth. Engulfing virtually every inch of its plot of land, its forty block-sized stories rising straight up form the lot line, its brooding shadow darkening seven adjacent acres of lower Manhattan, the Equitable eschewed the Woolworth's aspirations to filigreed beauty and sought only bang for the buck: what was the most building that could be erected for the least cost?

New Yorkers had finally had enough. In response, the city drew up the nation's first zoning law—one that would, among other things, determine the shape of its skyscrapers for the next half century.

With regard to the erection of tall buildings, the 1916 Zoning Law was all about building setbacks. According to Tauranac, "Buildings could start at the building line, but once they reached a certain height, they could continue upward provided they were set back from the line." A formula would be created to determine when setbacks took place, based on the width of the street adjacent to the building. In effect, a tall building was to take on the shape of diminishing boxes, as with a wedding cake. There was, however, one important zoning provision—a center tower, comprising no more than 25 percent of the plot, would be allowed to rise as high as the builder wished.

There were some restrictions on any such tower, of course. The structure had to be "architecturally treated" on all four sides. In other words, there could be no blank walls, as one would find at the rear of a building. Additionally, tower walls could be no closer than 100 feet to each other.

Central office towers, therefore, allowed for ego enhancement for developers who were determined to make a statement. True, to build too tall could be economic suicide (too many elevator shafts would take up too much rentable office space). There was an "economic height" to a skyscraper—a point at which, if more floors were added, the financial gain would turn negative. That, however, did not mean that such buildings would not arise. In the new decade dawning, self-glorification would often trump economics.

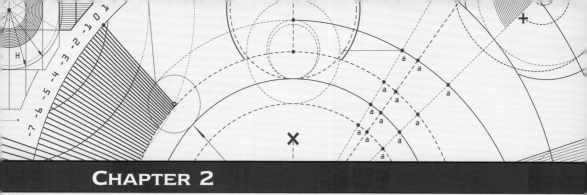

CHAPTER 2

The Race to Be the Tallest

Although Americans approached the third decade of the twentieth century with some apprehension, most were more than willing to leave the previous 10 years behind. The Great War (1914–1918) had been an unmitigated slaughter: 10 million solders were killed, 116,516 of them Americans. Immediately following the end of the war, the world suffered an influenza pandemic that took 50 million lives. Americans were not spared: 675,000 perished. With the 1920s now upon them, citizens clearly had had enough. The high and the low, the rich and the poor, were quick to turn inward to seek relief from world concerns. They wanted to live and let live; they wanted to have fun.

Morals, it seems, were the first to go. Flappers—women who dressed provocatively—took the lead by bobbing their hair, going out clubbing, drinking bootlegged alcohol, and living a less-inhibited lifestyle. The decade soon became known as the "Roaring Twenties."

New ways of living, and living it up, were based on heightened prosperity. Having expanded to meet the Great War's needs, American industry (despite a brief hiccup) continued to flourish after the war, fed by massive raw material reserves and high tariffs (the latter designed to keep competing foreign goods out of U.S. ports).

Consumer spending reflected the boom times. Higher salaries, plus the willingness to purchase on credit, meant more of everything, particularly for the middle class. Cars, refrigerators, radios, telephones, and all manner of consumer goods were "forced" on willing buyers through massive advertising. Due to mass production, the price of many industrial goods plummeted. The average car, which had cost $850 in 1908, fell to $290 in 1925. The Ford Motor Company was soon producing its Model T every 10 seconds. By 1927, Henry Ford had sold 15 million of the all-black cars.

At the same time, more fruits and vegetables entered the American diet—all the better to keep those flapper figures trim. Vitamins became the new health rage. Jazz-age jargon and slang were on everyone's lips, specifically among the urban "in" crowd. Young women were often referred to as *broads*, *bunnies*, *canaries*, *dolls*, and *the cat's meow. Jellybean, blind date, upchuck,* and *the real McCoy* were the "cool" phrases being spoken.

New York City was full of all the "jazz" of this Jazz Age. In 1928, according to the Merchants' Association of New York, as reported in *The Empire State Building: The Making of a Landmark:*

Using a twelve-hour day, more than fourteen couples got married every hour. The city's population of 6,056,000 consumed 2,659,632 quarts of milk and 7,000,000 eggs a day, eating a total of 3,500,000 tons of food a year, or about 1,000 pounds per person. More than 190 persons picked up the telephone receiver every second, and each day, 1,700,000 telephones were used to make 8,233,000 calls. Normally, there were 23,628 taxicabs in daily service, and on every business day, more than 500,000 persons arrived by train.

Those train travelers, heading for Manhattan, came mostly from surrounding New York boroughs, such as Queens, the Bronx, and Brooklyn. In 1927, the city, with its 5,528 square miles of territory, was spreading out. Residential areas were moving horizontally; commercial zones, however, were moving vertically.

Land values drove the economics of building taller and constructing skyscrapers. From 1900 to 1925, assessed values in New York had risen from $2.22 billion to $6.72 billion, an increase of close to 13 percent a year. It made economic sense to build upward in the business districts of Manhattan, both downtown and midtown. It also made personal sense: To own a skyscraper, especially if it could be the tallest ever, would promise not only a strong financial return but powerful bragging rights as well.

EGOS SOARING

According to Neal Bascomb, upon completion of the 309-foot World Building in New York in 1890, architect Harvey Wiley Corbett recalled, "Architects said nothing would be higher; engineers said nothing could be higher; city planners said nothing should be higher, and owners said nothing higher would pay." Architects, engineers, city planners, and owners rushed ahead, in the first decades of the twentieth century, bent on proving Corbett wrong. By the late 1920s, thanks to the likes of developers Walter Chrysler and George Ohrstrom, Corbett's prediction would all but evaporate.

Chrysler, born in 1875 in Wamego, Kansas, always considered himself a mechanic first and a businessman second. That did not prevent him, however, from becoming one of the richest men in America. After a stint running the Buick Motor Company, he formed the Chrysler Corporation in 1925; soon after, he added Plymouth, Desoto, and Dodge to his car lineup. By 1928, the automobile mogul sought to branch out, or, more precisely, up. He yearned to build a skyscraper headquarters in the heart of midtown Manhattan. Additionally, he insisted that it be the tallest building in the world—even loftier than the 791-foot Woolworth Building.

This process would be repeated by George Ohrstrom, a young man who achieved the position of bank president at 31 years of age. He had been a wartime aviator in World War I, and in the 1920s he was one of the most aggressive and powerful land developers in Manhattan. It was in the city—in the financial district— that Ohrstrom announced, on April 8, 1929, his plans to build a 64-story skyscraper at 40 Wall Street for the Bank of Manhattan Company. Such a building would challenge the proposed height

THE MAKING OF AN I-BEAM

In a steel-framed building, columns and beams form a metal cage to support floors and nonbearing walls. The columns are the vertical pillars that bear the building's weight, transferring it to bedrock. The beams are horizontal supports that link the columns and carry the floors. Although many shapes have been tested since steel-frame construction took hold, the I-beam, which resembles a three-dimensional uppercase letter *I*, has proven the most effective.

The I-beam consists of two parallel plates called *flanges* joined by a perpendicular plate called the *web*. Such a dual-flange/single-web form has a high strength-to-material ratio. As Jim Rasenberger wrote in *High Steel*, "The I-shape puts the most steel exactly where the piece needs to be strongest. Step onto a beam, the greatest stress will be on the top of the beam, which will squeeze together under your weight (compression) and at the bottom of the beam, which will pull apart under your weight (tension). The center of the beam will experience very little stress. Most of the steel, then, is concentrated on the top and bottom of the beam in the form of flanges, while little is wasted on its center."

of the Chrysler Building, and it would be ready for occupancy on May 1, 1930.

Two megabuilders going head-to-head to build the tallest office structure in the world would, of course, need architects with the vision to give them edifices equal to their soaring egos. Such architects were found in the likes of William Van Alen for Chrysler and Craig Severance for Ohrstrom.

Both architects had been partners at one time. Severance & Van Alen, Architects, had, in the midtwenties, achieved considerable critical and financial success. Van Alen was the creative force, the dazzling designer with an eye for style and form. Severance was the "suit," the guy who—though an architect—was more comfortable managing the business and wooing clients.

I-beams are formed at a steel plant by rolling a "bloom" of steel—a bulk raw material like a huge log in a sawmill—into an *I* shape. The rolls in the blooming mill, through which the bloom must pass, have deep grooves. In each successive set of rolls, the bloom is forced more and more into the shape of the finished I-beam. Thus, the rolling mill squeezes the bloom into shape. Alfred Morgan, in *The Story of Skyscrapers*, described the final forming process dramatically when he declared, "Writhing and trembling as if in fear of the terrific stress it is about to endure, the partly finished shape plunges again and again through the rolling mill, each time being squeezed a little more into its final shape and thickness."

I-beams and other structural steel shapes, once formed, are sent to the "bridge shop," where they are cut to exact lengths and pierced with rivet holes before being shipped out to a job site for use. An I-beam weighs from 10 pounds per linear foot to more than 300 pounds per foot. Such beams can, in turn, be built into trusses or girders that weigh more than 100 tons.

The race to build the tallest skyscraper in the world produced the Chrysler Building, a structure that combines the influences of art deco and automobile design. Walter Chrysler, an automobile tycoon, insisted on "a bold structure, declaring the glories of the modern age," and decorated parts of the exterior with hubcaps and hood ornaments from his cars.

Despite what seemed a perfect complementary relationship, the partners eventually split and became bitter rivals for the rest of their lives. In 1929, they were in full battle mode to see who could raise their client's building the highest.

By the time the architects sat down to design for their developers, a new, powerful architectural form had materialized. Neo-Gothic still prevailed in some quarters, and a few architects insisted on adornment wherever possible. Yet, art deco—first popularized at a French fair in 1925—soon came to define all manner of product style. The new aesthetic was characterized by sleek, streamlined forms that conveyed elegance and sophistication. Art deco reflected the machine age and based its design on industrial elements: locomotives, cars, and even household appliances. This style manifested itself in an architecture that was smooth, linear, and modern.

Although Severance's Bank of Manhattan Building displayed aspects of art deco design, it was the Chrysler Building that took the new style to the top, literally. From the start, Van Alen used fascinating automotive touches to highlight the building's automotive roots. Such design motifs as hubcaps and eagle gargoyles (representing hood ornaments) were to grace the building in classic art deco mode. At the top would sit a crown of stainless steel, a seven-layered dome that would reflect the sun for miles around.

Would the Chrysler Building be the tallest? Would it outdistance the Bank of Manhattan Building? As both structures rushed to completion, it was anyone's guess which one would win.

SECRET SPIRE

"The tower should grow out of the lower masses surrounding it," Van Alen said of his Chrysler Building design, as reported in *Higher*, "and it should terminate in a crowning feature that is a natural and logical development of the tower itself, not merely an ornament placed on the top of the tower." To that end, Van Alen designed a *cupola* (dome) to cap his building, the likes of which had never been seen. Representing the shining sun of progress and created with reference to the automobile, the chromium nickel, steel-facing peak, with its numerous triangular windows, would act as the crown of New York. It would be an art deco statement that none could top. It would be distinct.

More important, it would be tall. In September 1929, as the four sides of the long, tapered dome closed in on one another, it seemed clear just how high Van Alen planned to stretch his building—861 feet. The architect, however, had left an opening at the very top, a hole through which a flagpole could be raised from within. His rival, Severance, soon got wind of this plan and concluded that the needle would add 60 feet to the structure. The designer was not about to be outscaled.

Severance flew back to his drafting board to add a flagpole of his own, 50 feet in height. It would be enough, Severance was sure, to propel the Bank of Manhattan Building to a record height. In September, the downtown edifice topped out at 927 feet, taller than any office building anywhere—though shorter, by 59 feet, than the Eiffel Tower.

It was Van Alen who had the last say, however. The architect had indeed planned to raise a "pole" from within the dome, but it would be a lot taller than Severance (or anyone else) suspected. Weighing 27 tons, his spire's exact height was a well-guarded secret—even Chrysler did not know just how tall it would reach. Furthermore, the steelworkers who would build and erect what Van Alen called his "vertex" were unaware of exactly what they were constructing. The whole project was to be kept a mystery. Then, at the last moment, the spire would reveal itself like a "butterfly from its cocoon."

On October 16, all was ready. The five sections of the vertex had been lifted up within the dome and riveted together. "To hoist the vertex into position, the steelworkers had built an outrigger platform that projected over the four sides of the seventy-fourth floor," Bascomb reported. "First they secured temporary extensions to the floor on each side and then lashed down planks so they had room to step around as they maneuvered the twenty-seven-ton vertex into place."

Then it was crunch time. Bascomb continued:

> The men had to erect the vertex 860 feet in the sky, raising it up through the fire tower and securing it to the dome's top while moving quickly about the narrow cantilevered platform that offered space for one misstep, but definitely not two. A gust of wind or the snap of a cable threatened to send the vertex pitching headlong into traffic below. . . . Balancing an elephant by his trunk on top of the building would have been an easier proposition.

In 90 minutes, start to finish, the vertex was up and secure. The Chrysler Building, now standing 1,046 feet high, was the tallest structure in the world. Chrysler had won the race; his building had reached higher than any other. Unfortunately, the automobile titan had but little more than a year before he himself would be outdone.

THE EMPIRE BOYS

Al Smith—normally a jovial, backslapping, outgoing, and upbeat fellow—was, in late 1928, not very happy. Having just been soundly defeated in his bid for the U.S. presidency by Republican Herbert Hoover, the Democrat (and former governor of New York) not only was washed up politically, he also was unemployed. The "happy warrior" needed a job.

Smith, born in 1873 in an east-side tenement located virtually under the Brooklyn Bridge, grew up dirt poor. By the time he turned 15, Smith—the son of Irish Catholic parents—had quit school to work full-time as a truck driver's helper at the Fulton Fish Market. It was not long, however, before Smith took a liking to politics, and in 1903 he was elected to the New York State Assembly. Fifteen years later, running as a reformer, Smith was elected governor of the Empire State.

But now, unemployed as of January 1, 1929, and with only $6,000 a year for a pension, Smith needed work. He turned to his friend and confidant—and the man whom he had hired to run his failed presidential campaign—John Raskob. Maybe Raskob—who was wealthy beyond all reason and had once said, "Anyone not only can be rich but ought to be rich"—would have a job for the ex-governor.

Raskob was born in 1879 in Lockport, New York. At the age of 21, he went to work as a bookkeeper for Pierre S. DuPont, the gunpowder king. Raskob, with his quick, agile mind, rose high in the DuPont organization, and by 1913 he was advising his bosses on the purchase of stock options that he himself was quick to take advantage of. General Motors seemed like a good bet, and when Pierre DuPont later became its chairman, Raskob followed as vice president and chairman of the finance committee. It was not long before Raskob was a millionaire many times over.

According to Tauranac, "Raskob and Smith by then [1928] were friends, an odd couple to be sure, as unlike each other as two men could be. . . . But they both had risen from humble origins. . . . Both were quick studies, adept at mastering the details so that the big picture naturally came into focus, and both were enormously successful in their own fields." Raskob (the shy money man) and Smith (the people person) were a combination that could go far, especially in the New York real estate market of the late 1920s.

It is difficult to determine just when the two men got together to build the Empire State Building. According to one account, Smith and Raskob were out to dinner one evening at the Lotos Club. Smith had gone to the men's room with a friend and begun to recount his money woes; he did not know how he was going to make ends meet. Raskob entered a moment later and, overhearing the conversation, said, according to Landmark, "Don't worry, Al, I'm going to build a new skyscraper—biggest in the world—and you're going to be president of the company."

Looking for a new challenge, former governor of New York Alfred E. Smith *(above right)* was hired by his friend John J. Raskob *(above left)* to oversee the construction and management of the Empire State Building. Raskob, an executive at General Motors, wanted his new structure to eclipse the Chrysler Building, which was owned by his rival Walter Chrysler.

It is a good story but one of doubtful validity. Nonetheless, Raskob's vision came to pass. Together, Smith and Raskob would set forth to outdo Chrysler and construct the largest and tallest office complex in the world—they would build the Empire State Building.

BUILDING AMERICA NOW

TWO PRUDENTIAL PLAZA

Location Chicago
Architect Loebl, Schlossman, & Hackl
Height 994 ft.
Materials Reinforced Concrete, Aluminum, Limestone
Completion Date 1990

Two Prudential Plaza—consisting of two buildings, one of which was completed more than a half century ago (1956)—offers office workers and visitors a superb view of Lake Michigan. The first tower, One Prudential Plaza, was for 10 years Chicago's tallest building when it topped out in 1955. Considered one of the most modern post-World War II commercial structures, the 600-foot tall rectangular building had, at the time, 30 automatic elevators that were considered the world's fastest. The building also includes one of the largest parking lots, built within. Two years after it opened, One Prudential Plaza had attracted over a million visitors to its forty-first-floor observation deck.

Tower Two, completed in 1990, extends skyward to 994 feet. It consists of a parallelepiped on a square base with successive cutbacks that work their way to the top, which is characterized by an octagonal pyramid covering. The tapered upper portion recalls New York's Chrysler Building of 1929. The building's reinforced-concrete structure is covered with a facade of pink granite and reflecting gray glass.

"CLASS A" CONSTRUCTION

Al Smith was to be paid $50,000 a year as president of what would become the Empire State Building Corporation. Robert Raskob would garner the financing to erect a building. But where should it be built? When the Bethlehem Engineering Corporation defaulted on its second of two cash payments for the Waldorf-Astoria Hotel property purchased at Fifth Avenue and 34th Street, the opportunity arose to buy a choice site. A syndicate, headed by Louis G. Kaufman, was formed to do just that. In summer 1929, Kaufman proposed to Raskob that he become a principle stockholder in the development corporation, which he did.

Bethlehem Engineering, under the presidency of Floyd Brown, had previously hired the architectural firm of Shreve, Lamb, and Harmon to design a mixed-use, massive art deco, 50-story building for the Waldorf-Astoria property. On August 29, 1929, Al Smith announced the creation of the Empire State Building Corporation, which would build not a 50-story hulk, but a 1,000-foot-high, 80-story, "Class-A" (above average in design, construction, and finish, and having a superior location) office tower—the tallest building in the world. Shreve, Lamb, and Harmon would be retained to create the new design.

Who would actually build the Empire State Building, in retrospect, seemed an easy choice. Starrett Brothers & Eken, the firm that built the Bank of Manhattan Building at 40 Wall Street, was the premier skyscraper builder in the city. They specialized in large-scale projects, bringing them in under budget and, just as important, ahead of schedule. To get the Empire State contract, however, the firm would have to compete for it. Starrett Brothers & Eken would have to sell themselves and present their case.

The construction company was the last of five to make its pitch at a meeting to decide who would win the lucrative deal. "Contrary to popular conception," William Starrett told Empire State Building Company officials, as quoted by author Carol Willis in *Building the Empire State Building*, "the principal function of the general contractor is not to erect steel, brick, or concrete, but to provide a skillful, centralized management for coordinating the various trades, timing their installations, and synchronizing their work according to a predetermined plan, a highly specialized function the success of which depends on the personal skill and direction of capable executives."

If that did not get the committee's attention, they were certainly awakened by Starrett's response to Smith's follow-up question. "How much equipment do you have on hand?" the ex-governor wanted to know. "None, not even a pick and shovel," declared William Starrett, as quoted by Tauranac. "Gentlemen," the builder went on, "this building of yours is going to present unusual problems. Ordinary building equipment won't be worth a damn on it. We'll buy new stuff, fitted for the job, and at the end sell it and credit you with the difference. That's what we do in every big job. It costs less than renting secondhand stuff, and it's more efficient."

Ultimately, Starrett Brothers & Eken got the job. They would build the Empire State Building.

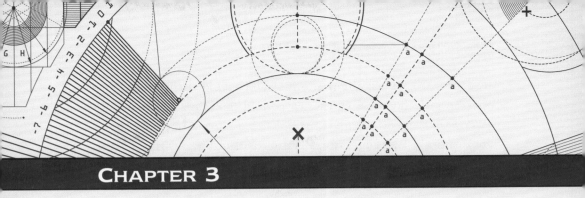

CHAPTER 3

Demolition

To construct a 365,000-ton structure (the eventual weight of the Empire State Building) would require a mantle-like foundation. Fortunately, the building's developers chose Manhattan, specifically midtown, in which to build. New York rises up as it does because of what exists below its surface. If one wanted to build tall in the early twentieth century, New York—sitting on a 450-million-year-old slab of metamorphic bedrock known as schist—was the place to do it.

Two large concentrations of mica-based schist exist near the island's surface. One is in lower Manhattan, and the other is in midtown. Where the schist is too far below the surface, such as in Greenwich Village (with an average depth of 260 feet), it is not possible to build high because it is too difficult to reach the schist upon which a building's foundation must rest. In lower and midtown Manhattan, schist is quite near the surface—in some locations no more than five feet down. When the Empire Boys dug for bedrock, at the corner on Fifth Avenue and 34th Street, they hit solid stone at 38 feet below basement dirt and gravel. Workers continued on to the 40-foot mark. True, crews would wind up carting off an amazing 28,529 truckloads of earth, rock, steel, and old Waldorf-Astoria Hotel debris to get to the glittering schist. But once there, developers were on firm ground. They would be ready to move up.

Geologically, the choice of the Empire State Building site was sound—but did it make sense economically? Was midtown the best place to plant a 1,000-foot-high, 2.1-million-square-foot "Class A" office tower in 1929?

In the last half of the nineteenth century, immigrants from all over Europe, particularly Eastern Europe, pressed

Manhattan schist, the bedrock of the New York skyline, was formed 450 million years ago after a series of continental shifts. Because of the varying depths of schist throughout the city, skyscrapers are built in clusters where the rock is closest to the surface. *Above*, a slab of exposed schist in Manhattan's Central Park.

through Ellis Island to settle in New York's Lower East Side. Tenement apartments in the area became so crammed with workers slaving away in their hot, cramped quarters, the district was soon declared one of the most densely populated concentrations on Earth.

By the turn of the century, garment work had spread north, into loft (factory) buildings around Washington and Union squares and up Fifth Avenue to as far north as 23rd Street. "Fifth Avenue was already said to have the heaviest vehicular traffic of any street in America," declared Tauranac. "The continued erection of tall buildings, especially of loft buildings catering to the garment industry, it was said, would naturally increase this congestion."

But there was more to it than traffic. Referring to the Save New York Movement, begun in the early 1910s, Tauranac continued, "Realtors and retailers of American-born stock or those of more recently arrived German-Jewish stock, began a public relations blitz to put a stop to what they regarded as an invasion of objectionable trades that employed undesirable immigrant minorities, mostly Jews from Eastern Europe."

As a result of efforts by the Save New York Movement and, later, the Fifth Avenue Association, by 1929 a section of Fifth Avenue—from 32nd to 59th streets—had become a protected area for high-class department stores and specialty shops. Fifth Avenue was to become the nation's high-class emporium, and it was here that the Empire State Building would rise.

By 1929, however, the area was already flooded with office space: 20 million square feet between 34th and 59th streets. Approximately 1.5 million square feet, or 13.3 percent, were vacant. Looking ahead a few years, those numbers were expected to grow to 7.5 million square feet and 28.8 percent, respectively. "Great caution should be exercised in selecting sites for and in designing and planning for new office buildings during the next few years, particularly in the midtown section," said realtor Loring M. Hewen, as quoted by Tauranac.

The Empire Boys paid little heed to such advice. They would build, and right in the heart of midtown Manhattan.

WALDORF-ASTORIA: BUILT TO LAST

Before anything could be constructed, however, something would have to be deconstructed, torn down, and carted away. It would not be easy, cheap, or quick to demolish the grand old Waldorf-Astoria Hotel. Indeed, it would take nearly five months, cost $900,000, and, by most accounts, present a great danger to those involved. Yet, down it would come, even though—when erected—the hotel had been built to last.

TORCHING THE WALDORF-ASTORIA

The steel-framed Waldorf-Astoria, built between 1892 and 1897, actually contained heavier columns and beams than a building of the same size would have if built in the 1930s. There was no way such a frame could be pounded down or cut apart with power saws. The Waldorf-Astoria would have to be torched—that is, cut apart—using oxy-acetylene blowpipes.

Such torches, used to weld metals together since around 1900, can with slight modification be used to cut apart metal effectively. The torch burns a mixture of oxygen and acetylene gas. The gases, contained in separate tanks, are fed to the torch through separate rubber hoses and mixed in proper proportions at the torch head. The flame produced can reach 6,300 degrees Fahrenheit. Because steel melts at approximately 2,300 degrees Fahrenheit, it will quickly give way to the oxy-acetylene flame.

By replacing a standard welding blowpipe with a cutting torch, what is normally used to weld metal together can be used instead for demolition. The cutting blowpipe is essentially a welding blowpipe that is modified to provide an additional stream of pure oxygen under pressure. It is the added oxygen that actually cuts the metal.

"Promptly following the first announcement of plans for construction of the Empire State Building, a motor truck drove through the wide door of the Waldorf-Astoria—the door at which presidents and princes, rulers of state, and the uncrowned kings and queens of society had been received," Geraldine B. Wagner declared in her book *Thirteen Months to Go: The Creation of the Empire State Building.* "The truck, like a roaring invader, thrust its great bulk into the lobby where surely such an intruder never had been seen before. It churned across the floor, then turned and roared down 'Peacock Alley,' that proud corridor lined with gold mirrors and velvet drapes. The end of the Waldorf had come."

The process of cutting involves first creating a red-hot spot on the steel column or beam to be cut. The oxygen jet is then turned on and directed against the metal.

According to Alfred Morgan, author of *The Story of Skyscrapers*, "The action is so rapid that a narrow slit or 'kerf,' as it is called, is quickly burned through the steel, in far less time than the most powerful saw could accomplish the same result. The process is really a chemical one and should not be confused with the mere melting of steel itself, which would be infinitely slower. In fact, what actually takes place is a very concentrated form of rusting, the slower natural form of which is familiar to everyone."

Using an oxy-acetylene torch, quarter-inch steel can be cut at the rate of at least 100 feet per hour. Steel that is 8 inches thick can be severed at about 17 feet per hour. No saw or drill could even approach these rates.

Oxy-acetylene torches sputtered their way through the Waldorf-Astoria as quickly as saws cut timber. In some cases, the old rivets were taken out with the white-hot flame; at other times, the girders were cut in two.

Actually, the end of four Waldorfs was at hand. The original Waldorf Hotel, constructed in 1892, was, according to *Building the Empire State Building*, "a semi-wall bearing type of construction with cast iron columns and wrought iron floor beams and girders." The hotel averaged 12 stories and had a capacity of 4,100,000 cubic feet. Because the heavy, ornate masonry structure was a bearing structure, it would have to be demolished with great care; otherwise, it might collapse uncontrollably.

The Astoria section of the Waldorf-Astoria was built in 1897 and in places stood 16 stories, or 216 feet, high. Though it featured late-Victorian architecture, with massive exterior masonry walls, the 7,245,000-cubic-foot building had a steel-frame construction. Older demolition methods, in which materials basically are pounded until they collapse, would be used on the masonry portion of the building. More modern techniques, which used torches to burn steel apart, would follow.

The Waldorf Annex, a four-story building also constructed in 1897, would have to come down as well. The annex contained 665,000 cubic feet of space and—like the Astoria section—it had a steel-frame construction.

Finally, the Astor Court Building, an annex built to provide office space for the hotel, would also have to go. Also featuring a steel-frame construction, its 900,000 cubic feet contained relatively little ornamentation on its exterior nonbearing walls.

It would take a workforce of more than 600 men, laboring day and night, to demolish the Waldorf-Astoria site. Demolition actually began on September 24, 1929, and all masonry and steel were completely torn down to sidewalk level by February 3, 1930. By March 12, 1930, the last stone—buried below the building's old machinery foundations—was removed.

"A contemporary poet described in poignant verse the air of lonesomeness and sadness surrounding a 'house with nobody in it,'" *Notes on Construction of the Empire State Building* declared in its introductory chapter on the wrecking of the Waldorf-Astoria Hotel. "Whenever he passed it standing alone in solitude he always felt it deserved a better fate than desertion because it had been a 'home that had sheltered life.'"

Regardless, as part of their contract to erect the Empire State Building, Starrett Brothers & Eken had agreed to clear the site, take down what was there, and get rid of the remains one way or another. The old Waldorf-Astoria Hotel would have to make way for the new—the Empire State Building.

A DANGEROUS UNDERTAKING

Professional destroyers, wreckers, and those in the business of taking down what was once painstakingly erected have plied their trade since the time of Babylon. As recently as the late nineteenth century, firms contracted for the task of destruction actually paid for the privilege of taking a building down, as long as they could salvage what remained. The wreckers would make their profit by selling the used copper, zinc, brass, lead, and any other metals they found, all of which were recycled for industrial use. Fixtures—both plumbing and electrical—could be sold for reuse. It was often a lucrative business.

By the 1920s, however, the job of demolition had changed. It had become harder, and thus more costly, to dismantle better-constructed buildings. Furthermore, the demand for secondhand hardware diminished as new, modern, art deco styles emerged. Wreckers were soon forced to charge for their work—as much as $200,000 per job, according to Tauranac.

It seems that even used lumber had become a challenge for the destroyers. Tauranac offered an apt illustration:

> Wreckers had even lost the sale of small and otherwise useless pieces of wood to the "wood merchants," who had previously paid as much as $10 a load. These entrepreneurs had hauled the discarded wood to their basement workshops where "wood-chucks" cut it up into kindling sizes and sold the recycled wood by the bag to tenement dwellers to burn in their woodstoves. With that outlet dried up in the twenties, wreckers and builders

frequently disposed of the wood by hauling it at $15 a load to swamplands, where, in what seems the making of an ecological mistake, it was burned.

It would cost nearly a million dollars to dismantle the Waldorf-Astoria and cart away what remained. Starrett Brothers & Eken was up to the task, however, and they, along with selected subcontractors, began tearing the building apart on September 24, 1929. A few days earlier, Al Smith—ever the publicity man—took to the roof of the hotel and declared, before

Piece by piece, workers removed bricks and the steel frame of the Waldorf-Astoria, careful not to disrupt the crews above them or drop anything on the people below. Construction of the Empire State Building began after the removal of scrap material from the old buildings. *Above*, construction of the Empire State Building reaches about 16 stories.

assembled photographers (according to Bascomb), "Gentleman, stand back while I start the real work of demolition." The ex-governor then pulled a cable, yanking down a 10-foot section of copper ornament. "The northward march of progress has reached the heart of the city," Smith continued. "I feel sorry to see this historic old building torn down, but progress demands that it must go. . . . On this site will rise the largest office building in the world—eighty stories tall."

Demolition would now proceed one story at a time. Safety was the key issue, and masonry was the problem. The material simply could not be blasted away and allowed to fly in all directions. Of course, cutting up the steel frame would be no easy task either. "Any skywalker will tell you that tearing down a steel building is even more dangerous than building one," Wagner explained. "The demolition must be done by hand; if achieved too rapidly or with too much force, destabilization can result in a disordered and reckless collapse."

Demolition was, indeed, a risky business. The workers were in danger—crawling around as they must, ever mindful of what was not only beneath them but also above—and so were pedestrians. The more prudent ones took long detours around deconstruction sites. According to Tauranac, the insurance on the Waldorf-Astoria teardown amounted to 35 percent of the total cost.

PRY AND CUT

Of all the ironworkers, the erectors—the column-climbing connectors—are literally and figuratively at the top, both on the job and in the hierarchy of job status. When it comes to deconstructing, however, it is the barman, wielding his tempered steel pinch bar, who the other wreckers look up to. According to Tauranac, "The barman was the one worker who was madcap enough yet cool-headed and skillful enough to drive the toe of his pinch bar into a wall that he might have been standing atop and loosen the timber or bricks below him without causing the wall or himself to fall down." Barmen concentrated on demolishing the sidewalls and floors of the Waldorf-Astoria. They were paid a dollar an hour for their labors, which was a decent salary in 1930.

Once the masonry and terra cotta were pried apart and broken up, the pieces were dropped through wooden chutes located inside the building. The chutes extended from where the wrecking was being done directly to hoppers on the main floor. From there, Mack 5-ton trucks, equipped with special 24-inch sideboards, hauled debris to scows at the East River and 32nd Street. If pieces were too large to heave into scows, they were carted to local land dumps.

All this tearing down of brick and clay created the potential for a daily "dust storm" at the work site. Merchants—and the public in general—were inconvenienced enough by all the noise and commotion. Dust on department store display merchandise, on clothes, and in one's eyes was to be avoided if at all possible. Plenty of water, sprayed liberally about, helped keep dust down and tempers cooled.

Once the structural steel was exposed, steelworkers with acetylene torches took to cutting it apart—the reverse of their normal duties as steel constructors. "The steelworker would take the torch with its fine blue tip, swing it like a wand over the beam he was going to cut, and turn up the oxygen," Tauranac wrote. "The flame would shoot out, and, as it ate into the steel, fiery particles would cascade down (when the torches were not being used to cut apart steel, some workers cavalierly used them to light their cigarettes)."

Construction records show that 17 oxy-acetylene torches were used in the demolition of the Waldorf-Astoria. The torches required no less than 802,000 cubic feet of oxygen and 195,000 cubic feet of acetylene gas.

All told, 14,615 tons of structural steel and miscellaneous scrap iron, 36 tons of scrap copper, and 8 tons of brass, lead, and zinc were removed from the hotel site and sold. One item that was not sold, however—but was instead given away—was wood. By early 1930, the economic effects of the stock market crash of October 29, 1929, were being felt, particularly in urban areas such as New York City. Unemployment was rising, businesses were closing, and the Great Depression settled upon the country. Partially as a publicity stunt, but also from genuine concern, Al Smith decided to have all surplus wood from the Waldorf-Astoria cut up into stove-size pieces and hauled out, on a daily basis, to a vacant lot on West 30th Street. The six truckloads a day would

BUILDING AMERICA NOW

KEY TOWER

Location Cleveland
Architect Cesar Pelli
Height 948 ft.
Materials Reinforced Concrete and Steel
Completion Date 1991

The tallest building between Chicago and New York, the Key Tower, can be seen from as far as 20 miles away. Designed by the famous American architect Cesar Pelli, the nearly 1,000-foot structure takes at least its pyramid top from William Van Alen's Chrysler Building of the late 1920s. The office tower is considered a classic example of postmodern architecture. Constructed on a rectangular plan, a parallelepiped volume with traditional setbacks rises above the base as the building reaches for the sky. The pyramiding top is, in turn, topped out with a sharp spar.

The base of Key Tower is faced with stone, and the upper portion of the skyscraper is lined with steel panels. The central core, which houses the elevators and various facilities, is a steel structure, as is the building's perimeter. The Key Tower is an excellent example of the marriage of concrete and steel in modern skyscraper construction.

provide free kindling for those who could not afford to purchase wood or coal. More than a few New Yorkers relied on Smith's wood to get them through the winter.

TWO JOBS IN ONE

To save building time, the Starrett brothers decided to do something extraordinary and bold, if not downright crazy—they would attempt to start construction on the Empire State Building while still demolishing the Waldorf-Astoria Hotel. In other words, the construction company would actually begin building while still in the process of tearing down. It was a bizarre thing to do, but Starrett Brothers & Eken had attempted it before, successfully, during the construction of the 40 Wall Street Manhattan Building. They felt they could do it again at Fifth Avenue and 34th Street.

On the Wall Street site stood a 14-story building that would have to come down before the new skyscraper could ascend. While clerks continued to type and file in their offices, foundation workers for the new building chipped away at the basement floor. Three weeks later, when the tenants finally moved out, razing the building began in earnest. Demolition and foundation teams worked simultaneously: one tearing down and the other seeking to set the foundation.

"It was a filthy job and dangerous as well," Bascomb wrote of the foundation men at their task. "While the buildings above them were being demolished, they had to work under cramped, low basement ceilings and slog through boiling quicksand and half-darkness. Hydraulic jacks boomed like cannon fire as they struck the steel cylinders. Sweat soaked their shirts and overalls, and half the time they sloshed around in ankle-deep water."

A similar technique would now be used as the Waldorf-Astoria came down and the Empire State Building rose up in its place. Even before the last of the grand hotel had been demolished, 600 men—working in two shifts (one day, one night) of 300 each—began digging the skyscraper's excavations. Three cranes, three derricks, four steam shovels, and four compressors were used. The general excavation was started on January 22, 1930, and finished on March 17, 1930.

Once the site was cleared to approximately five feet below the old sub-basement floor of the Waldorf-Astoria Hotel, actual pier-hole excavation could begin. Thirty-eight feet below the original basement level, the builders found what they were after—Manhattan schist, or bedrock. Now 210 holes (8–10 feet square) would have to be carved out of dirt and rock and filled with concrete pier footings. The footings would carry the building's supporting steel column loads to bedrock schist.

To clear a hole to bedrock, blasting of the above-schist rock often was required. As Tauranac described it:

> One workman drilled a hole in the stone. Another took the sticks of dynamite from small wooden boxes and, using a rod, pushed them one by one into the hole. . . . Everyone except the operator of the nearby steam shovel then backed off. The steam shovel operator covered the hole with a large steel mesh mat. . . . A muffled *thunk* would be heard, the carpets would surge up, a cloud of smoke and dust would come from the hole, and the very ground beneath would shake. Then the workers would return to prepare for the next blast, and the cycle would continue.

In total, 463 cubic yards of earth and 4,992 cubic yards of rock were excavated from 210 pier holes. The holes were then filled with concrete—3,744 cubic yards in all.

The tops of the concrete piers were next reinforced with I-beam grillages. The grillages, set at right angles and buried in concrete, would concentrate the load from a column base across the width of the pier. The 210 massive steel columns that would pull the Empire State Building skyward were set upon the piers. By March 29, 1930, what was to be the tallest building in the world was ready to rise up from its pier footings and reach for the sky.

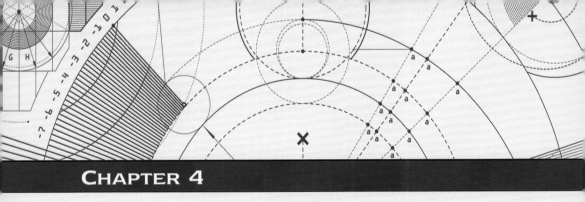

CHAPTER 4

Empire Rising

The architectural firm of Shreve and Lamb (later to add Arthur Harmon) was no stranger to the Waldorf-Astoria site in midtown Manhattan. When the Bethlehem Engineering Corporation bought the hotel in late 1928, it instructed the architects to come up with the design for a massive, 50-story, mixed-use art deco behemoth. The building, which had 2 million square feet of rentable space, was to devote its lower 25 floors to shops and lofts and its upper 25 to offices. In a unique feature, the structure would contain vehicular ramps, which would lead from 33rd and 34th streets to a motor truck terminal in the basement of the building, where trucks could be unloaded directly at the elevators.

The Empire Boys would have none of it. Upon acquiring the property, they agreed to retain Shreve and Lamb, but they directed the architects to return to their drawing boards. The new owners required something less massive yet higher. They wanted a building of modern skyscraper design. Smith and Raskob demanded an office building where form would follow function.

The term, "form follows function," is credited to Louis Sullivan, one of America's pioneering architects and considered by many the creator of the modern skyscraper. Born in 1856, Sullivan entered the Massachusetts Institute of Technology at the age of 16. At 17, he found his way to Chicago, where—for a short time—the young drafter worked for William Le Baron Jenney, the architect who erected the "cage designed" Home Insurance Building in 1885, the world's first skyscraper. Breaking away from traditional design, Sullivan soon hit upon the idea whereby a building should be designed according to its function. Its form, derived from its function, would then follow naturally.

Such buildings, devoid of ornamentation (which was considered superfluous), were said to be appealingly honest. They were simple and functional—and, of equal importance, they were practical and commercially viable.

With column-frame steel construction, functionality could, at last, reign supreme in building design. Tall buildings could now rise up. Furthermore, with only curtain walls wrapped around a structure, windows could be much larger. With large windows, more light would penetrate interior spaces. Interior walls, now no longer required to bear the structure's load, could be made thinner. More rental floor space would result.

All this modern skyscraper design would, it was hoped, lead naturally to the construction of a practical, moneymaking building. That is the type of building that Smith and Raskob told Shreve and Lamb to come up with in 1929. While the architects were at it, they might as well design the tallest structure in the world.

Doing so, reaching higher than ever before, would be possible in this case primarily because the Empire State Building site was so large. At 197 feet long on Fifth Avenue and 425 feet on 33rd and 34th streets, the lot—nearly two acres in size—was twice that of a typical plot in midtown Manhattan.

Even though New York City's zoning laws would allow the Empire State Building to rise up high from street frontage—13

Believing that the design of the structure should come after its purpose, Louis H. Sullivan's *(above)* practicality focused on constructing towering buildings that would serve as commercial space. He used the phrase, "form follows function," to describe this new style of architecture, a philosophy that inspired the modern skyscraper and the Empire State Building.

stories on Fifth Avenue and about 17 stories on the two streets—before setbacks were required, in the interests of keeping the neighbors happy the owners were willing to scale back. "Although our building will contain some 3,000,000 square feet of rental space," Smith told the *New York Times*, "we are taking about 300,000 square feet less than the amount permitted under the zoning laws for a building plot of such tremendous size." The finished Empire State Building design called for only five floors to be constructed over the entire ground area. After that, setbacks would begin.

SPEEDY DESIGN

Plot size was not the only factor that influenced the Empire State Building design. Of even greater consideration would be the need for speed: the demand to get the structure up and open for rent-paying tenants as quickly as possible. As Paul Starrett would later declare, when reflecting on his career (as noted by Carol Willis), "Never before in the history of building had there been, and probably never again will there be an architectural design so magnificently adapted to speed in construction."

Smith and Raskob insisted that the Empire State Building be completed and ready for occupancy by May 1, 1931. The architects and builders would have to demolish the Waldorf-Astoria, erect the world's tallest building, and have tenants in place in a mere 18 months, or about 630 calendar days—an unprecedented undertaking.

Why this demand for speed? And why May 1? What was so special about that date? In the New York real estate market of the 1920s, May 1 was moving day. It was on this date that commercial leases commenced. For anyone whose lease was up on April 30 and who wanted to move, May 1 was the right time—the only time—to do it. On that date, Manhattan was clogged with movers and moving vans clearing out old offices and refurnishing new ones. Thus, if a building was not completed and ready for occupancy on May 1 of a given year, a whole year's rent could be lost. May 1 was a completion date that could not be missed.

To make it happen as fast as they could, a team approach to design and construction was essential. No one entity—architect, builder, or developer—could possibly do it alone. As Carol Willis observed, "From the outset, the owners, architects, and builder worked in committee to develop the building's program. This method avoided mistakes in design and costly delays in

SAFETY FIRST

Although six workmen died constructing the Empire State Building, there is no contesting the fact that the builders took every precaution to protect workers and pedestrians during the 18 months it took to demolish the Waldorf-Astoria and erect the tallest building in the world. Throughout construction, a 50-man safety crew roamed the building site, their only function to spot unsafe working conditions and immediately correct them.

Perhaps the overall safety philosophy of management was best expressed by the author of the notebook published in *Building of the Empire State Building* (edited by Carol Willis, director of New York's Skyscraper Museum): "A careful Superintendent appreciates, first of all, that he is not only the custodian of the property of his employer, but in a higher moral sense, he is also the protector of the lives of those working under him and of the public coming in contact with his building operation."

Safeguarding pedestrians was, indeed, of paramount importance. To that end, a sidewalk overhead, constructed of tubular scaffolding with noncombustible flooring, was put up even before the Waldorf-Astoria came down. As Alfred Morgan, author of *The Story of Skyscrapers*, put it, "For the passer-by and the workmen going in and out of the ground floor this is the principle protection against any objects which might fall on the outside of the building from the floors above. Nails, bolts, wire, construction." Paul Starrett would write later, in praise of the committee approach: "I doubt that there was ever a more harmonious combination than that which existed between owners, architects, and builders. We were in constant consultation with both of the others; all details of the building were gone over in advance and decided upon before incorporation in the plans."

In due time, basic design guidelines were derived. As William Lamb explained, as quoted in *Building the Empire State*

small fragments of brick or stone, to say nothing of larger objects, can do serious damage when they fall from any appreciable height."

A number of specific safety precautions were put into effect to protect workers. Some were unique to the construction of the Empire State Building. Following are a few examples:

* Ladders were discouraged; stairways were used instead.
* All shafts were protected with wire mesh.
* Material hoists were constructed so that the platform could be locked to the floor where material was unloaded.
* Unused openings were protected with guardrails.
* Three apron scaffolds, at different floor levels, extended completely around the building.
* A close watch was kept on the pipe scaffold around the mooring mast tower to prevent icicles from forming and falling into the street.
* Special attention was paid to prevent the throwing of rivets toward the outside of the building. A missed rivet could mean death to someone on the street below.

Clearly, no expense was spared to ensure safety on the job during construction of the Empire State Building.

Building, "The program was short enough—a fixed budget, no space more than 28 feet from window to corridor, as many stories of such space as possible, an exterior of limestone, and a completion date of May 1, 1931, which meant a year and six months from beginning of sketches."

On October 3, 1929, the design team, who had gone through 16 previous iterations (sketches), decided on "Scheme K" as the final design. The Empire State Building would be a tower, with a center core of elevators, toilets, shafts, stairs, and corridors. The sizes of the floors would diminish, and the elevators—which numbered 64 at the lobby floor—would decrease in quantity as the building rose. To achieve maximum light and air from the outdoors, windows would open and no office would be deeper than 28 feet.

The basic Empire State Building design was said to have derived from a simple pencil. As the story goes, Raskob, meeting with Lamb, pulled a thick pencil out of his desk drawer and held it up. "Bill," he declared, as quoted by Geraldine Wagner, "how high can you make it so that it won't fall down?" Eighty-five stories was the answer.

ECONOMIC HEIGHT

Yet eighty-five floors would be a stretch—technically and, particularly, economically. Elevators were the main problem, though not because they would compromise structural integrity. Elevators required a great deal of time and took up gobs of space. Of course, tall buildings need elevators; the higher the buildings, the more elevators are required. After all, folks are not going to want to wait around to be taken aloft (25 to 30 seconds is the delay time most busy tenants and customers are willing to tolerate).

Elevators, too, are space intensive. As Tauranac put it, "In a traditional skyscraper, where all elevators start at the lobby floor, the elevator banks occupy the lion's share of the lower floors, and valuable space is sacrificed that could otherwise be rented. The higher the tower goes, the more space is sacrificed."

Furthermore, to be successful, a tall office structure like the Empire State Building would have to provide direct elevator service. Transfers would need to be limited or, better yet, eliminated entirely. It was all a matter of efficient vertical circulation. The developers figured that more than 15,000 workers and visitors would need to be taken up and down the building in the half hour at the beginning and ending of each workday. A minimum of 58 passenger elevators would be required to do that.

As designed, the Empire State Building would, in turn, need both local and express elevators. At the time, the maximum elevator speed allowed by the city code was 700 feet per minute. That, however, would be too slow for the high-rise elevators to take passengers to their destination in an acceptable time. To get to the eightieth floor in little over a minute, elevators would have to travel at 1,200 feet per minute. Such high-speed elevators were a technical reality in 1930 but were not, at the time of construction, legally operable.

The Empire State Building designers immediately applied for a zoning change that would allow them to use the faster elevators. Taking a gamble, they installed the speedier versions in hopes that by the time the building opened they would have the right to run them at top speed. By the middle of June 1931, the new zoning law had taken effect, and passengers were immediately sped swiftly up and down the building. Those who alighted on the eightieth floor, however, and wanted to reach the eighty-sixth floor observation deck, would have to transfer to one of two final, short-shaft elevators to take them to the top.

Getting people up and down an 80- or 85-story building was technically feasible, but did it make economic sense to build that high? All buildings have what is known as an *economic height*, an elevation at which—as the developers continue to add floors—they begin to lose money. Carol Willis put it this way:

> The price of land is a major factor in the complex real-estate equation known as *economic height*, which is the number of

stories a developer must build to reap the maximum return on the money invested. Taller towers require more foundation, structural steel and windbracing, mechanical systems, and, particularly, more elevators and shafts. At some point for every skyscraper, rents for the extra stories do not justify the additional costs, and the owner will make more money by erecting a *shorter* building: that number of stories is the building's economic height.

For the Empire State Building, the magic economic height was 80 stories, the number of floors served by the main bank of elevators. Floors 81 through 85, originally intended as office space for the developers and also as service spaces, actually made no economic sense. Then again, building the Empire State Building was not all about economics; ego was at work as well.

WALLED IN

Externally, the Empire State Building would need to be wrapped in a protective curtain wall. Unlike the all-glass structures popular today, a fair amount of masonry gave ubanites a sense of strength and permanence. Never mind that masonry or stone panels just hung there, supported by the building's steel skeleton. A rock-solid look was still in vogue in the fourth decade of the twentieth century.

The walls of the Empire State Building would need to enclose as large a space as possible, because the larger the area of a building floor, the less exterior wall per square foot is required. Additionally, the less outer wall needed to do the job, the less the expense. Exterior walls—with their windows, limestone, spandrels, and metal trim—can be the most costly part of any skyscraper.

If a floor plan, for example, is 40 feet square, it contains 1,600 square feet of space (40 X 40 = 1,600). The exterior wall is 160 linear feet (40 X 4 = 160). Dividing 1,600 by 160 results in 10 square feet for each foot of wall. However, if the floor plan is 80 feet square, there is now 6,400 square feet of space (80 X 80 = 6,400).

Grateful for work during the Great Depression, men learned to ignore their fears as they built the 85 floors of the Empire State Building. *Above*, a steelworker straddles a cable during the construction atop the Empire State Building.

The exterior wall is larger, at 320 feet (80 X 4 = 320), and the new size results in 20 square feet for each foot of wall (6,400/320 = 20). The larger plan gives more square feet of office and utility space for a given wall size—twice as much, in fact.

Indiana Limestone was the architect's choice for sheathing the Empire State Building. Plans called for no less than 200,000 cubic feet of limestone made up, for the most part, of identical slabs 4 inches thick.

The building would include 6,500 double-hung metal windows. Importantly, the window frames would be set into their openings such that the frames covered the edges of the flanking limestone. Thus, the stone did not require finishing at its edges, which saved money.

Placed vertically between the windows would be cast-aluminum spandrels with classic art deco motifs, such as stylized lightning bolts set in a chevron-like pattern. The average

BUILDING AMERICA NOW

PETRONAS TOWERS

Location Kuala Lumpur
Architect Cesar Pelli & Associates
Height 1,483 ft.
Materials Reinforced Concrete, Steel, and Glass
Completion Date 1998

For eight years, the tallest skyscrapers in the world, the Petronas Towers—located in the capital city of Malaysia—represented the true fusion of modern, reinforced concrete construction and Eastern aesthetics. "Introduced" to Westerners in the popular film *Entrapment*, starring Sean Connery and Catherine Zeta-Jones, the towers truly have taken their place on the world stage. Designed by American architect Cesar Pelli, the towers incorporate the Islamic use of the symmetrical geometry of squares and circles. The buildings are designed to resemble minarets.

In addition to gaining their structural integrity from concrete (not steel), the Petronas Towers—according to Antonino Terranova in his book *Skyscraper*—consist of a "facade [that] meets requirements of ecological compatibility (made necessary by the tropical climate) through several layers and devices. . . . The approach and its aesthetic effects are radically different to the traditional and elementary curtain-walls made of metal and glass panels that were typical of the International Style." The Petronas Towers are truly unique.

spandrel was 4 feet, 6 inches high and 5 feet wide. Each 130-pound spandrel would fit between the top of one window and the bottom of the one above it.

Finally, running vertically the length of the building's facade would hang stainless-steel mullions, sandblasted to a velvety surface. Such mullions, as Tauranac points out, were not only a critical design element but also an important construction factor:

> Rolled in sheets half an inch thick, the mullions generally came in one length—the height of one story—and, depending on their placement, in one of two widths, ten or twenty-two inches. In addition to contributing to the upward sweep of the facade, the mullions were a critical element in the ease of construction. Like the window frames, they too covered the joints.

The Empire State Building's exterior, then, would consist of a repeating series of stainless-steel mullions, limestone-faced piers, cast-aluminum spandrels, and double-hung metal windows. Behind the curtain wall would be an inner wall of common brick (10 million bricks would be needed) to keep the building's interior warm and fireproof.

READY TO GO

On April 7, 1930, massive steel tower foundation columns—210 in all—began arriving on-site, at Fifth Avenue and 34th Street. Nothing like them had ever been produced before.

"COLUMN TO SUPPORT 5,000 TONS ON EMPIRE STATE BUILDING," read the *New York Times* headline. The article declared, "A giant steel column, weighing a ton for each foot of its length and reported to be much larger than any ever before used in office building construction, is being fabricated as the 'master' link in the steel framework which will carry the burden of the weight of eighty-five stories in the Empire State Building."

The columns themselves were made of built-up sections. The standard sizes of rolled steel section were not adequate for the tremendous loads at the base of the building. Thus, reinforcing plates had to be riveted on at the factory. The *New York Times* continued, "The width of measurements of the column are 3.6 by 2.4 feet, irregular, the equivalent of five square feet. The section is designed to support a weight of 10,000,000 pounds, or 5,000 tons."

It would take 350 men just to erect the columns for the Empire State Building. Such columns, which typically arrived at the building site in two-story-high sections, had a splice at the bottom, beam connections in the middle, and beam connections and a splice at the top, according to Donald Friedman in *Building the Empire State Building*.

The bottom section of the tower foundation columns, which were 15 feet, 8 inches long, weighed 44 tons; the upper section, which weighed about the same, was 33 feet long.

By late May 1930, all of the foundation columns were in place and the Empire State Building's frame was set to ascend. Unfortunately, just as the building was ready to reach up, the American economy was crashing down. The nation was in a depression, and the construction industry, particularly in New York City, was collapsing.

In the first year that followed the stock market implosion of October 1929, overall construction in the United States dropped 50 percent. Massive unemployment took hold. People in all walks of life became desperate, often forced into doing what only months before they never would have dared. As one New Yorker said, as quoted by Wagner, "The Depression was terrible. People were livin' in cardboard boxes. . . . I seen people on the street beggin' for pennies, sellin' whatever they could find—apples, fountain pens, somethin' they picked up or stole. . . . Basically they were honest people, but they stole to survive. They'd steal clothin' off a rack on Orchard Street, pants, shirts, shoes."

Amid the desperation and unemployment of the Great Depression, the announced construction of the Empire State Building— which during its rise to the sky would at times employ close to

3,500 men—was like a thunder blast heard across the city. Those lucky enough to find work erecting the tallest building in the world felt that its existence was a godsend. They clung to their jobs like a lifeline, even as, racing to see the job done in record time, they hurried themselves to an unemployed future.

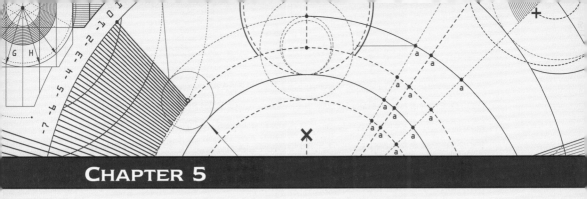

CHAPTER 5

A Story a Day

Though the headline "THE ACROPHOBIC NEED NOT APPLY" was never posted at any job site, those who wished to erect skyscrapers—that is, work to frame the Empire State Building—could not have suffered from an abnormal dread of high places. Never mind that 23 percent of Americans are so afflicted; if one wanted a job in a rising gang, fitting-up gang, or riveting gang in 1930s steel-frame construction, he needed a steady foot and a clear sense of where he was at all times.

The work was about never forgetting to remember. An iron-worker had no right to lose focus. "If an office worker sitting at his desk happens to lose himself for a few moments in a dreamy reverie, it's no great matter," Jim Rasenberger, author of *High Steel*, observed. "No one dies. Ironwork isn't like that. The construction site of a steel-frame building is a three-dimensional field of hazards. Hazards come from above, from below, from every side, and a man up there has to stay alert to these hazards many hours a day. Spacing out can be lethal."

Anyone who wanted employment as an ironworker first had to pass a physical aptitude test. One was required to, at a minimum, climb a 15-foot column, walk across a narrow beam, and slide down the opposite column. As Rasenberger noted, "The test tends to weed out the frail and the fat. It also weeds out acrophobes. Why an acrophobe would apply to be an ironworker is a mystery, but it happens occasionally."

Falling, of course, is the paramount fear all ironworkers have. Plunging is always a possibility; it can happen every time a man shinnies up a column or takes a walk out onto a six-inch-wide beam. "Falling is the thing he is always striving not to do, and the moment he stops striving not to do it, he puts himself in danger," said Rasenberger. "Gravity lies in wait. All it needs is a false step, an ankle that turns in, a slight stumble, an instant of an imbalance or idiocy or just plain spaciness. Falls account for 75 percent of ironworker fatalities."

One does not have to drop from 50 floors up, it should be noted, to face a deathly encounter with the earth below. In a study done in 2000, it was found that half the ironworker falling fatalities occurred in falls under 30 feet. A fifth of fatalities happened when the ironworker dropped from a distance under 15 feet.

"Ye, gods!" wrote builder William Starrett in 1928, as reported by Rasenberger. "If there ever was an experience to bring to the human body its sense of helplessness and despair, its agonies and terrors, it is the sensation felt by one who has not had training when he suddenly finds himself out on a narrow beam or plank, high above the ground and unprotected by a hand-hold of any kind."

Yet they came by the hundreds to work, to construct the tallest building in the world. The Empire State Building would have no trouble finding ironworkers, Swedes, Danes, Finns, Norwegians, Irishmen, and, of course, Mohawks, ready and eager to frame its skeleton.

Why not? The pay, at least before the Depression fully mani-fested itself, was great. The average worker on the skyscraper earned $15 a day, an excellent rate in the early 1930s. A hoisting engineer, however—a member of the alpha raising gang—could command $2.31 per hour, or $18.48 for an eight-hour day; double pay was offered for overtime and Saturday work. Although Al Smith boasted that all the work done on his building was accomplished during the day, he was stretching the truth. Many a laborer began his workday at three thirty in the morning, while most of New York slept, and did not finish until four thirty in the afternoon—13 hours later.

Of course, unlike today, an ironworker was paid only for the actual hours worked. Bad weather, broken machinery, delayed materials, and time lost between jobs meant no pay. Still, there were hours to work and there was money to earn.

THE GANG'S ALL HERE

No ironworker worked alone. Everyone belonged to a gang, even if it was a gang of only two. There were approximately a half-dozen such construction gangs, and all of them worked on rais-ing the Empire State Building.

"Their faces are different," wrote Alfred Morgan in *The Story of Skyscrapers*, first published in 1934. "They are the ironwork-ers, and nowhere else except on the framework of a new bridge will you find the same sort of tireless, courageous, nimble, ox-strong men. They never loaf and they use their brains as well as their muscles."

If one gang member called in sick, the rest of the gang took a day off—without pay. Each member of a gang knew the rhythms, modes, moods, and ways of his fellow members. In some cases, failure to work as a well-oiled machine could not only jeopardize efficiency, it could also be life-threatening.

At the apex of the construction industry, figuratively and liter-ally, was the rising gang. These gangs, which consisted of five men, were the ones that actually erected the steel: the columns, beams,

Steelworkers *(above)*, mostly immigrants and Mohawk Indians, had to be physically and mentally disciplined in order to work at great heights. Laboring night and day, more than 3,000 men managed to construct four-and-a-half floors each week until the Empire State Building was completed.

and girders. Using derricks, they guided pre-hole-punched steel into place. "Like an elite military unit, it's the rising gang that goes in and captures territory," said Rasenberger. "By the time others arrive, the raising gang is off to claim the next level of altitude."

In a rising gang, two men—the connectors—are key. As the Empire State Building's frame rose up (at times at more than four floors a week, or close to a story a day), the connectors were the ones to make the initial coupling of columns and beams. Once they snatched the swinging steel, they "set" it in position and "hung" it with one or two temporary, high-strength bolts.

"Two hundred, five hundred, a thousand feet up, these fearless, daring workmen, loaded down with twenty or thirty pounds of nuts and bolts in their pockets and a heavy wrench in their belt, shinnied monkey fashion up the steel columns," wrote Morgan. "They strode across a four inch 'needle' beam with nothing between them and oblivion except their uncanny nerve and fine sense of balance."

Right on the connector's tail is the fitting-up bunch, divided into plumbers and bolters. The former tighten up the pieces with guy wires and turnbuckles and make sure they are in plumb (alignment). The bolters add more temporary bolts.

In the days of cast-iron construction, the nuts and bolts put in place by the rising gang would have been tightened and left permanently to do their job of joining the building's metal frame. Steel-framed structures are not bolted, however; they are riveted. Driven red-hot into a prepunched hole, when a rivet cools it "freezes" to become one with the metal it joins. Rivets are better than nuts and bolts.

A rivet gang consisted of four men, often referred to as the heater, the catcher, the bucker-up, and the gunman. At any one time, there were 35 to 40 rivet gangs working on the Empire State Building. An expert gang could drive a rivet a minute, or more than 500 in a regular workday.

In operation, the heater lays a few wooden planks across a couple of beams to form a base for his portable, coal-burning forge, which heats the rivets. The heater, sensing when a mushroom-shaped rivet is red-hot, picks the rivet off the coals with a set of tongs and tosses it—sometimes up to 75 feet—to the catcher who catches it in a metal can. The bucker-up, in the meantime, has unscrewed one of the temporary bolts and removed it, leaving the hole empty. The catcher now removes

MAIL DROP

Today, the Empire State Building has its own zip code. It also has its own post office. When the building was designed in 1931, as many as 20,000 tenants were expected to require mail service. Letters and packages would have to travel up and down all 86 floors. To ensure that the upper floors would be as valuable as the lower (in terms of rental space), they would need to be serviced as well as any other. To that end, the architects specified modern Cutler Mail Model "F" mail chutes to run, top to bottom, throughout the building.

According to rediscovered 1930s notes on building the Empire State Building:

These chutes are arranged in pairs, and by means of a device which can be operated only by post office officials, the chutes are closed on alternate floors, dividing the mail and reducing the risk of congestion by overcrowding. In case one of the chutes in any pair is in need of cleaning or repair, it can be closed throughout its entire length, and the mail service continued temporarily by means of the other.

The mailboxes that appeared on every floor—all 396 of them—were made of aluminum and bronze and were richly ornamented. Placed in a single line, they would measure approximately a mile.

Nothing, it seems, including mail delivery, was left to chance by the Empire State Building designers. They thought of everything.

the rivet from his bucket with a set of tongs and shoves it into the hole. He then steps aside. The bucker-up man, using a tool called a dolly bar, places it over the head of the rivet and holds it there. The gunman, wielding a 35-pound, pneumatic jackhammer, places the gun against the rivet stem. The piston within strikes at 1,000 blows a minute, smashing—in 15 to 20 seconds—the semimolten metal into a button flush against the steel.

Heat, toss, insert, and smash—the process was repeated over and over again as the Empire State Building's frame, all 60,000 tons of it, was stretched to the heavens. All in a day's work.

THE FOUR "PACEMAKERS"

In fact, this repeat process, assembly-like method of construction is what characterized the erection of the Empire State Building. "Given the design of the Empire State," said Paul Starrett, as quoted by Tauranac, "their job was one of repetition—the purchase, preparation, transport to the site, and placing of the same materials in the same relationship, over and over." Instead of the parts moving, as on a regular assembly line, with the Empire State Building it was the workers who moved, each doing his specific job—laying bricks, window glazing, installing pipes, or spreading concrete—over and over again.

Key to the entire operation was the work of what the contractors called the four "pacemakers." The erection of steel; the setting of concrete floor slabs (arches); the installing of metal trim, aluminum spandrels, and windows; and the placing of exterior limestone determined the speed of construction. Other trades—bricklayers, electrical installers, plumbers, lath and plasterers, tile setters, and so on—could follow with their work only after the four pacemakers had completed their tasks.

Steel erection was, of course, critical. Nothing could happen until the framing was in place. By its progress, the speed of construction was gauged. "Columns commence to stand up like magically produced trees, those farthest from the derrick first, then here and there a panel of steel," observed William Starrett, as quoted by Carol Willis. "Almost as you watch, you notice the connecting of the panels, and in a day or two a whole tier of beams."

For all its strength—typically 50,000 pounds per square inch—steel will, under load, squash (compress). When the Empire State Building was topping off, workers found that the eighty-fifth floor was more than six inches lower than expected. "The first-tier columns measured immediately after erection would be the same length they were in the shop, but as each floor was built, and the 'dead load' accumulated in the form of the floor slabs, the exterior walls, and the interior partitions and plaster, the columns became steadily shorter," reported Friedman in *Building the Empire State Building.*

For those who set the exterior limestone, the discrepancy was negligible; a mere one-sixteenth of an inch per floor is easily ignored. Yet, for workers who installed the elevators, critical adjustments had to be made before everything in the building would fit as intended.

Because there was no way to store steel beams on-site, their creation, fabrication, and transportation had to be planned and timed almost to the minute. It was said that, in some cases, steel arrived at the construction site—ready to be immediately hoisted up—just 80 hours after it was formed at the steel mills. When placed in position, some claimed it was still warm to the touch.

Concrete floor slabs, 4 inches thick, were poured throughout the 85 floors. The concrete, mixed with light cinder material, was reinforced with wire mesh every 2 inches. Each slab would span roughly 7 feet between beams. More than 62,000 cubic yards of concrete was used to form the building's arches. The exterior curtain wall, as has been seen, was made up of continuous limestone panels with a common brick backing, spandrel panels (also with a common brick backing), windows, and stainless-steel mullions.

With alpha construction workers setting the pace, the Empire State Building's 85 stories were completely enclosed by November 13, 1930—17 days ahead of schedule.

FED, PAID, AND DOUBLE-CHECKED

Early on, even before steam shovels cleared any Waldorf-Astoria rubble, it was apparent to Starrett Brothers & Eken that feeding their 3,000-plus workers every day was going to be a challenge. The men (carpenters, bricklayers, elevators installers, electricians, plumbers, trade specialists, inspectors, and foremen) had to eat. Not only would there be lunch, but such hungry guys would want their snack breaks.

Although some workers, left to their own devices, could be expected to brown-bag it, the vast majority would want to buy their food. How, it was asked, would it be possible to move thousands of laborers, even with temporary caged elevators in place, down to street level, into nearby eateries and restaurants, and back up to their work spots, all in the half hour typically allocated for lunch? Clearly, it could not be done.

Soon enough, it was decided that the men must be fed on-site, as close to their actual working stations as possible. To that end, Starrett Brothers & Eken decided to build cafeterias throughout the building as it rose, and to offer the concessions to a local restaurateur if he agreed to feed the men good food at a reasonable price. As the *Notes on Constructing the Empire State Building* declared:

> A high class restaurant operator, with three restaurants in the vicinity, was told he could have the privilege for a very nominal sum per month (enough to pay for light and power), if he would agree to have the builders construct for him, at the restaurants owner's expense, five lunch stands as the progress of the work required them. These lunch stands were built, when needed, on the 3rd, 9th, 24th, 47th, and 64th floors, and were completely equipped by the restaurant owner and remained in these locations throughout the life of the job.

With so many construction workers operating on different floors of the Empire State Building, Starrett Brothers & Eken developed some ingenious methods for feeding and paying their workforce. The construction firm contracted outside agencies to provide on site food service and to pay the crew on a weekly basis.

As a result, instead of scurrying to get out at noon when the lunch whistle blew, men walked to the nearest food stand and bought a good lunch of chicken salad, beef stew, beefsteak pie, frankfurters, and sauerkraut, for as little as 40 cents. Hot coffee, milk, near beer, soft drinks, ice cream, candies, cigarettes, and tobacco also were sold. The restaurateur, James P. Sullivan of Lord's Chain, was said to have made a decent profit, and during the life of the entire project not one complaint was received concerning the quality or price of the food served.

Paying 3,000 workers each week turned out to be a challenge, too. Every Friday, $250,000 in cash had to be correctly and safely doled out to workers at their stations throughout the building. Once the bank did its auditing and checking, pay envelopes—with each worker's name affixed—were given over to an armed service corporation. An armored car with five armored service men then drove to the Empire State Building. Each worker received his pay, right at his workstation, in cash.

How did the company know who was working where, and how much time they put in? They checked, often and thoroughly. According to *Notes on Constructing the Empire State Building:*

> During the day, field time checkers visit every man on the building; once in the morning and once in the afternoon and ask him to show his brass check. This gives four checks each day on every man; when he reports for work at the time office, during the forenoon, during the afternoon and when he turns in his check each night. On Friday morning (pay day) he receives an aluminum check bearing his number, in addition to his regular brass check. He presents the aluminum check to the paymaster when he receives his pay.

The job of running this huge operation, which called for an on-site workforce of 3,000-plus employed by the general contractor and some 40 subcontractors, fell to the job superintendent. Such a person, it was said, possessed a forceful and aggressive personality, tempered with the qualities of tact and infinite patience. It goes without saying that he needed to have a complete knowledge of building construction.

BUILDING AMERICA NOW

CONDÉ NAST BUILDING

Location   New York
Architect   Fox and Fowle
Heigh   810 ft.
Materials   Reinforced Concrete
Completion Date   1999

The Condé Nast Building, located in Times Square, represents the revitalization of the famous intersection at Broadway and 42nd Street. As a result of midtown Manhattan development in the 1930s and 1940s and the renewed interest in downtown in the 1970s, Times Square redevelopment meant going back to the city's original core. City planners chose the architectural firm of Fox and Fowle because of its record in designing ecologically sustainable buildings that are highly respectful of their environment.

The 48-story Condé Nast Building has two types of facades: The west side of the building is a curtain wall of steel and glass, and the east facade is made of brick to complement the elegant setting of Bryant Park.

The building has received recognition for its exceptional technological and ecological characteristics. According to Antonino Terranova in his book *Skyscrapers*, "Energy is produced using photovoltaic cells and a specifically coordinated system to control the temperature that, functioning in tandem with a wastewater system, cools the air and thereby minimizes consumption of polluting fuels."

HAZARDS OF THE JOB

Workers died building the Empire State Building. One rumor had it that no fewer than 100 lives, one for every floor, were sacrificed in the mad, unrestrained rush to build the tallest skyscraper in record time. An only slightly more restrained claim put the number at half, 48 deaths. The truth was less shocking and more noteworthy. Six workers lost their lives at the construction site, reflecting a safety record applauded for years afterward. "It is an extremely regrettable fact that this happened," wrote the author of *Notes on Construction of the Empire State Building*, "but these lives were lost through accidents which occurred due to the normal hazards of modern buildings and certainly not, as charged, to inhuman indifference and neglect."

One mechanic, in a clearly avoidable death, stuck his head in an open elevator shaft to see where the elevator was. Another worker was hit by a truck while sawing a plank. A third laborer ran into a blast area. A fourth stepped off a scaffold. A fifth fell down an elevator shaft. A sixth, an ironworker, was struck by a hoist.

Then, on July 11, 1930, Miss Elizabeth Eagher was struck in the ankle by a piece of broken ironworker's plank while crossing 34th Street west of Fifth Avenue. Though initially she sustained only a fractured ankle, Eagher later died as a result of blood poisoning.

Such falling debris injuries, and the possible lawsuits they could cause, were a constant concern for Starrett Brothers & Eken. While the men toiling outside the building façade worked from scaffolds, or "duck walks," suspended from the floor above, below them hung catchall scaffolds. Two such scaffolds were in place around the perimeter of the tower at all times. One, set under the stone and brick setters, had solid planks and wire mesh. The second, set about 15 feet below the first, was there to catch light objects that might fall within the intermediate floors. As noted by Tauranac, "To show the worth of the catchalls, a foreman who escorted a reporter around the

As the building's framework rose above the city skyline *(above)*, rumors of construction workers falling to their deaths loomed over the site. Despite the apparent danger, construction at the Empire State Building was mostly safe, with only a few deaths attributed to human error.

construction site asked the reporter if he had noticed a bolt that had dropped to the scaffolding. 'That little chunk of iron is worth about $10,000. If it had dropped to the street, instead of right here, and if it had hit someone, they—or their relatives— would have got the money.'"

For workers inside the building—plasterers, electricians, plumbers, painters, and so on—life, protected from the elements, was a bit less hazardous. With internal hoists doing most of the heavy lifting, and with the temporary installation on every floor of a pushcart, 12-gauge industrial railway system to move materials quickly to a particular workstation, in a steady, predictable, and timely manner, the Empire State Building's steel-framed 85 stories (86, including the observation deck) climbed to completion on September 19, 1930.

That was not, however, where construction would actually stop. Eighty-five floors would make the new building the tallest in the world, outdistancing the nearby Chrysler Building—but only by a few feet. Something had to be done, the developers were insistent, to rise definitively above that meager disparity. The Empire State Building would have to climb still higher, and dramatically so.

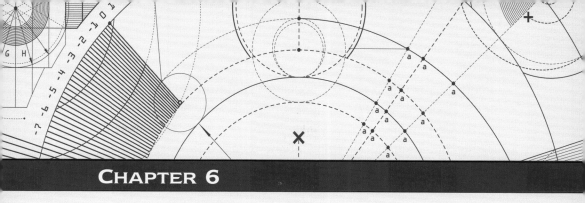

CHAPTER 6

Dangling Dirigibles

"What the building needs is a hat!" John Raskob was said to have declared upon pondering his height competition with Chrysler, so fervently pursued in late 1929. Although he had previously announced an elevation of 1,050 feet for the Empire State Building, it was but 2 or 3 feet above his rival's building. Such a slim margin was simply too slight to tolerate. The developer was afraid that Chrysler would pull a trick and hide within his spire a rod that could be stuck up through it at the last moment. A cartoon published at the time showed a building, similar to the Chrysler Building, with a caption that read, as quoted in *Higher*, "You see, this spike runs down the entire length of the building and if anyone builds a taller building we can up the spike and still be tallest."

Technically, more stories could, of course, be added to the Empire State Building. It might even be possible to take the building past the magic 100-story mark. The architects, however, were opposed. Moreover, additional floors would not pay. As it was, going from the original plan of 80 to 85 stories was going to be financially iffy. It already appeared doubtful that the top five floors could even be rented. Rising beyond that was no good.

Besides, more of the same—more floors to rent—would hardly be dramatic. Nothing about doing that seemed bold, adventurous, daring, or different. It was decided that, if the building were to have a hat, it must be distinctive and, quite unheard of in skyscraper design at the time, useful. In other words, the Empire State Building's additional reach would have to have a practical purpose.

"SMITH SKYSCRAPER TO HAVE DIRIGIBLE MAST TOWERING QUARTER OF A MILE ABOVE FIFTH AVENUE" screamed the *New York Times* headline of December 12, 1929. "A mooring mast for dirigibles with a built-in landing platform for transatlantic passengers will tower 1,300 feet, a quarter of a mile, above Fifth Avenue at 34th Street, when the new Empire State Building is finished, former Governor Alfred E. Smith announced yesterday," the *Times* reported. "Thus the structure will be not only the tallest building in the world, but the first to be equipped for a future age of transportation that is now only a dream of pioneers in aviation."

This was, indeed, bold, daring, and, most assuredly, unusual. Whether it was practical, or even feasible, was another matter.

Of the latter, it seemed Smith had little doubt. "Mr. Smith," the *New York Times* went on, "said the dirigibles would be warped to the mast by an electrical winch, much as an ocean liner is warped to its pier. A ship once moored can swing in the breeze and the passengers go down a gang plank to the elevator in the tower, he declared."

The ex-governor's plan was beginning to sound a bit far-fetched. Still, Shreve, Lamb, and Harmon, after consulting with leading dirigible experts, were assured that the steel frame of the Empire State Building could be strengthened sufficiently to withstand the pull of the greatest zeppelin in anything less than a 50-mile gale. Elevator facilities would be available through the tower to land people directly on the ground after completing their ocean trip, seven minutes after the airship connected with the mast.

Within a day of the announcement, Smith visited Secretary of the Navy Adams in Washington to ask for the aid of experts in mooring mast construction. Meanwhile, plenty of ordinary folks thought that adding a 200-foot mooring mast, even if it brought the Empire State Building to a technical 102 floors, was just plain nuts.

AIRPORT IN THE SKY

Airships (*dirigibles* in French, *zeppelins* in German) are lighter-than-air aircraft that can be steered and propelled through the air. They were all the rage in the 1920s. Passengers rode in a gondola (enclosed compartment) under the balloon. Filled with helium or hydrogen, such steel-framed "floating" transports could travel up to 80 miles per hour for thousands of miles without refueling. Considered as luxurious as any ocean liner (yet twice as fast), by late in the decade such airships were already traversing the Atlantic. Routes were planned for the West Coast, South America, and the Pacific.

Some airships were nearly as long as three football fields stretched end to end. In early 1930, in Akron, Ohio, the Goodyear Zeppelin Company was in the process of building a dirigible 785 feet long, the largest in the world. It would be ready by late August.

Airships, of course, had to dock. Traditionally, such mooring would take place in an open field, far from urban congestion. In this regard, New York presented obvious problems. At one time it was thought that several blocks in Manhattan would have to be razed, and a towering dirigible landing stage set, if the city was to be serviced by such ships. Clearly, though, knocking down blocks of New York buildings in the real estate boom of the 1920s was not going to happen. Smith, with his mooring mast proposal atop the Empire State Building, seemed to solve the docking problem.

To build such a mast, assuming that airships could actually use it, meant reconfiguring the top of the Empire State Building. The roof of the eighty-fifth floor would no longer be the summit. The roof would now become the eighty-sixth floor, with a glass-walled observation gallery. Then, from the center of the new top floor the rocket-shaped mooring mast would rise. As Tauranac described it:

> A thirty-five-foot square shaft of metal and faceted glass would rise 158 feet from the eighty-sixth floor to the conical roof atop the structure for the dirigible mast. The winches and control machinery would be installed at the base of the mooring mast; the cables, elevators, and stairs would be in the shaft; and the mooring arm would be housed under the conical roof.

Furthermore, at the very pinnacle there would now be two additional observation decks. One, at the one hundred and first floor, would be a glass-enclosed circular room with a 33-foot diameter. One floor up, on the one hundred and second floor, would be an open observatory with a 25-foot diameter, ringed by a low protective wall. As Tauranac pointed out, "The primary purpose of the platform was not so much to wow visitors with the view but to serve as the boarding area for the anticipated dirigible passengers."

Could such a mast, a tower, even be built? Was it structurally possible? Yes, but the entire frame of the Empire State Building would first have to be reinforced to take the added stress of a mooring mast that, in turn, would be tugged by the load of wind-tossed airships. "The mooring mast had to have strength enough to withstand a horizontal pull of fifty tons at its head," Tauranac noted. "It had to be constructed so that stresses resulting from that load and from wind pressures would be transmitted through the building to its foundation nearly eleven hundred feet to the entire frame."

Eager to outdo all other skyscrapers, John Raskob was soon presented with the idea to create a dirigible mooring mast *(above)* on the top floor of his new building. The dirigible was quickly becoming a popular form of transportation, as people could travel great distances in a short amount of time on an airship.

Al Smith claimed it could be done, that the steel frame of the structure could be made to withstand the pull of an airship as long as the wind blew at less than 50 miles per hour. The job of adding a mooring mast was estimated to cost about $750,000. On November 21, 1930, two months after the framing of the main building was completed, the top of the mooring mast "topped" out. Smith's airport in the sky, it seemed, was soon to be a reality.

FOLLY OF FOLLIES

"The looniest building scheme since the Tower of Babel," Tauranac called the idea of a dirigible mooring mast: "Folly of follies."

LEWIS HINE:
The Workman's Documentarian

Though he was 55 years old in 1930, Lewis Hine—a well-known and respected humanist photographer—went to great (and risky) lengths to do his job. Hired to photograph the construction of the Empire State Building from March 1930 to May 1931, Lewis often would climb out on the steel frames to get close-up shots of the construction workers. He took some shots from the end of a derrick cable that suspended him 1,000 feet above the ground. Hine, particularly interested in what Berman described as "the precarious interaction of man and machine, flesh and steel," concentrated his efforts on the dangerous nature of the workers' jobs. The iconic images we see of 1930s men at work (and at leisure) out on thin metal columns and beams high above the ground are Hine's legacy.

Beaumont Newhall, writing in *The Magazine of Art*, described a typical day in the "high-rise" photographer's life: "With the workmen he toasted sandwiches over the forges that held the rivets; he walked the girders at dizzying heights, carrying over his shoulder not a pocket-size miniature camera but a five-by-seven-inch view camera complete with tripod, or a four-by-five Graflex."

First, there was the considerable, not to be ignored problem of violent air currents plaguing the skyscraper canyons of Manhattan. "Anyone who bothered to ponder the mechanics of unloading passengers at such heights came away skeptical," Mitchell Pacelle, author of *Empire: A Tale of Obsession, Betrayal, and the Battle for an American Icon*, noted. "Tall buildings break breezes into incalculable currents. City streets act like chimneys. Roofs reflect the sun and generate minisqualls, turning the air turbulent and untrustworthy. How would the enormous craft, devilishly difficult to steer, reach the spearlike mast of the Empire State Building in the erratic winds?"

When the pinnacle of the Empire State Building had been reached, Hine had workers swing him out over the city from a crane to get the final, climactic shot he had been striving for the past six months. He described the moment in his own words, as reported by Geraldine B. Wagner:

My six months of skyscraping have culminated in a few extra thrills and finally achieving a record of the highest up when I was pushed and pulled onto the peak of the Empire State, the highest point yet reached on a man-made structure. The day before, just before the high derrick was taken down, they swung me out in a box from the hundredth floor (a sheer drop of nearly a quarter of a mile) to get some shots of the tower. . . . I have always avoided dare-devil exploits and do not consider these experiences, with the cooperation the men have given me, as going quite that far, but they have given me a new zest of high adventure and perhaps, a different note in my interpretation of industry.

Geraldine Wagner, author of *Thirteen Months to Go*, was even more incredulous in her view of the project. "When one considers that atop the Empire State snow falls up instead of down, it is easy to recognize the type of updraft that the dirigibles would have had to fight against to land, or even to remain motionless for the time needed to allow passengers to disembark."

Wagner raised another problem that Smith and his planners failed to consider, or simply ignored. "Dirigibles also required several ropes for handling rather than the single rope that was originally intended," she said. "When combining these logistics, the sheer danger of the possibility of millions of cubic feet of hydrogen gas exploding over a densely populated city deemed the mooring unusable."

Perhaps the most bizarre aspect of all was the expectation on the part of developers that passengers actually would be willing to step out of a wind-buffeted dirigible onto a long, swaying gangplank a quarter of a mile in the air. In retrospect, it appears that Al Smith had not given that issue much thought at all. There was a great deal, it turned out, that Smith had failed to consider.

The experts were even more skeptical about the mooring mast idea than the general public. True, the navy had agreed to "study" the problem for Smith. That did not mean, however, that they endorsed any plan to have dirigibles actually dock atop the Empire State Building. Naval officers concluded that the air currents set up by midtown skyscrapers would require continual trimming to the airship's keel level. That would mean throwing out ballast (water). "How would it be possible to dump tons of water on the streets below?" they wondered.

Finally, Dr. Eckener, commander of the *Graf Zeppelin* and chief operating officer of Zeppelin of Germany, expressed his disapproval. "The difficulties of mooring a great airship to a mast over New York City would be very great," he declared, as quoted in *The Empire State Building*. "The violent air currents up and down caused by your high buildings would, I think, make such a project almost impossible at this time. I would never try it with the *Graf Zeppelin*."

DOCKING GONE BAD

Though Dr. Eckener was not willing to attempt docking a dirigible to the Empire State Building, Smith still clung to the hope that doing so would become a reality. The navy never sanctioned the Empire State Building as a dirigible port, but it did attempt an airship "swipe" of the building in December 1930. The flight, made at the request of a motion picture newsreel service, had no official connection with the Empire State Building or the navy, and no actually docking was contemplated. The *New York Times* reported:

> Slowly and with its command on the alert lest the delicate fabric of its envelope be staked on the sharp spires of the tall buildings in the Pennsylvania zone . . . the semi-rigid dirigible J-4, auxiliary of the *Los Angeles* of the Lakehurst Naval Air Station, reconnoitered about the dirigible mooring mast atop the new Empire State Building at 3:15 P.M. yesterday [Tuesday, December 17], while thousands watched from the streets below. . . . A stiff wind was blowing as the dirigible hovered with throttled engines and approached the high tower and superstructure of the new building. In the cabin of the airship, Lieutenant S. M. Bailey, the commander, kept his hands on the controls and ballast releases in case a gust threw him too close to the near-by buildings.

Nine months later, on a September day in 1931, an actual attempt to dock—feeble and failed as it turned out to be—took place. A small, privately owned dirigible made its way to the Empire State Building with a long rope dangling from its bow. "The pilot jockeyed for position for about a half hour, or until the airship's ground crew of three could catch the rope," Tauranac reported. "They hung on to it for dear life, and the dirigible was made fast atop the mooring mast for three minutes, a maneuver that brought Fifth Avenue traffic to a halt. All the while a steeplejack was armed with a sharp knife, poised to cut the rope should it become fouled." Later, the pilot of the small airship was reported to have advised that the mooring mast could be used to land mail and express packages, an idea Smith was quick to adopt.

In what everyone acknowledged as an obvious publicity stunt, in late September 1931, Smith assembled a small group on the deck of the Empire State Building's one hundred and second floor. Along for the occasion was his partner, John Raskob. To promote the twenty-fifth anniversary of the *New York Evening Journal*, the Goodyear blimp *Columbia* would drop a 100-foot-long rope to the newspaper's building, where a bundle of newspapers would be tied to it. The blimp would fly to the Empire State Building to drop its rope in the hands of a waiting steeplejack. The ground crew's chief rigger on the one hundred and second floor would then grab the newspapers.

As the scheme unfolded, the rigger cried, "Hold my legs, somebody, in case I get pulled," as reported by Elizabeth Mann. With that injunction, Raskob wrapped his arms around the man and held him fast. The rigger finally grabbed the rope, cut it, and handed the bundle of newspapers to Al Smith. The first, and last, roof-to-roof airship delivery of newspapers had taken place.

With this final, ridiculous attempt at using the mooring mast, all pretense as to the practicality of the original plan was dropped. The rigging to be used for docking dirigibles had never been completely installed. The final installation was quietly postponed. The Empire State Building's mooring mast would have to find a new name and, along with it, more sensible uses than the one first envisioned.

OPENING DAY

On March 1, 1931, two months ahead of time, the Empire State Building was ready to receive tenants. The builders, Starrett Brothers & Eken, had done it: They had constructed the world's

BUILDING AMERICA NOW

BURJ AL ARAB

Location Dubai
Architect W. S. Atkins & Partners
Height 1,053 ft.
Materials Steel and Glass
Completion Date 1999

Burj Al Arab is the tallest hotel in the world and the only one, anywhere, to be given a seven-star rating. It does not actually have any rooms—guests stay in two-floor suites equipped with high-tech amenities. Designed by Scottish architect Jonathan Speirs, the Burj Al Arab, with its sailboat shape, has achieved worldwide iconic status as it sits on a manmade offshore island in the Persian Gulf—a "resident" of Dubai, United Arab Emirates. Begun in 1994, the hotel incorporates Middle Eastern architectural features such as spheres, domes, vaults, and arches. The hotel boasts the highest atrium in the world—54 stories to the sky.

Built on piles implanted 130 feet into the seabed, the steel-frame structure is formed by three huge piers that form a triangle. Two of the piers curve like arches, and the third goes straight up. Near the building's top is a circular heliport. Burj Al Arab is not for the common man; the sailboat skyscraper hotel is a refuge for only the privileged few.

largest office building ahead of schedule and, thanks to the price-depressing effects of the Great Depression, brought it in under budget—$40,948,000 (including land) versus an initial estimate of $50,000,000.

It had, indeed, been an impressive achievement, a credit both to the skilled trades that set steel, poured concrete, and wired the offices, and to the organizational genius of the general contractor. The official opening on May 1 brought unrestricted praise from all over the Empire State and declaration, time and again, of the singular construction accomplishments, especially with regard to speed.

The first steel columns were set on April 7, 1930, and the floors for 85 stories were all poured by October 6, 1930. Exterior metal trim was erected by October 17, 1930. The limestone facet was enclosed by November 13, 1930, and the building was completely ready for occupancy by May 1, 1931.

"As a rule," *Notes on Building the Empire State Building* declared, "this information was received incredulously, especially by foreigners, and when the truth became apparent, it was pronounced marvelous that the enormous quantities of material and equipment needed could be fabricated, shipped from the various sources—in many cases from foreign countries—and erected into a complete structure within a short space of time of one year."

On the cool, slightly hazy opening day, Al Smith—before a throng of well-wishers and the press—had his two grandchildren cut the red ribbon at the Empire State Building's Fifth Avenue entrance. The children were there, Smith explained later, as reported in the *New York Times*, because the building had been built "for generations to come down through the ages, and the two small children, with scarcely the proper understanding of just what was going on, were there to symbolize for all time to come that this building is to be a monument for generations to come."

With the ribbon cut, and the doors thrown open, the honored guests rushed to fill the Empire State Building's huge pink Famosa marble-faced lobby. "Visitors entering the Fifth Avenue lobby are immediately struck by the dazzling ornamental panel of bronze and marble with a likeness of the Empire State Building, as well as medallions symbolizing the crafts and trades that went into the building's construction," John S. Berman reported.

After 410 days of construction, Raskob's skyscraper was opened to the public in a grand ceremony on May 1, 1931. Crowds were impressed with the ornate art deco relief in the lobby, depicting the Empire State Building atop a map of New York State.

"Other wall panels display maps of New York and adjacent areas, with a gauge representing the direction in which the wind is blowing at the top of the building."

It was to this top—to the observation tower—that most folks now rushed. "There the guests viewed Manhattan Island and the metropolitan area from a new pinnacle," the *New York Times* reported. "Few failed to exclaim at the smallness of man and his handiwork as seen from this great distance. They saw men and motor cars creeping like insects through the streets; they saw elevated trains that looked like toys."

"At night, the scene was hardly recognizable as the same which greeted the daytime visitor," the *New York Times* declared in an accompanying article. "Beyond the immediate shadows of midtown Manhattan on the south a million windows glowed with light from the towers of the financial district. . . . Lines of lights and the dim, errant flicker from motor vehicles marked the streets, with Broadway as a kaleidoscope of flickering color."

Al Smith was having his day. More sobering times, for the nation and for the Empire State Building, lay ahead. But for now, on May 1, 1931, the entire world was eager to celebrate completion of the tallest structure ever conceived by man.

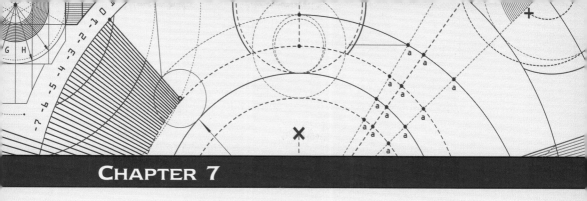

CHAPTER 7

The Empty State Building

In the speed of its assembly, the number of bricks it contained, and its innovative construction methods, the new colossus now open for business at the corner of Fifth Avenue and 34th Street in midtown Manhattan was, indeed, impressive. According to Geraldine Wagner:

★ It took 7 million man-hours of labor to construct the Empire State Building.

★ On the busiest day of its assembly, 3,439 laborers showed up for work.

★ If all the materials used in building the Empire State Building had been delivered at the same time, a train 57 miles long would have been needed.

★ One worker working every day would have had to put in 25 years to mortar the 10 million bricks used in the building.

★ To haul the Empire State Building's 200,000 cubic feet of limestone would have required more than 400 flatcars.

★ The building contained 1,172 miles of elevator cable.

★ Under the floors and in the walls of the Empire State Building ran 75 miles of main water pipes.

★ The building opened with a completely self-contained fire department.

★ For power and lights, 2 million feet of electrical wires snaked through the Empire State Building, equal to 380 miles.

★ The Empire State Building contained sockets for 350,000 lightbulbs.

Now, all that was needed were tenants—many of them—to fill the 2 million-plus square feet of rentable office space the building had to offer. There was a mortgage to pay, and the developers were anxious to start collecting rent money. Although Starrett Brothers & Eken had saved a bundle in construction costs due to the lower wages and material costs that resulted from the worsening Depression, the other side of the coin was about to show itself. Because businesses were going under at an alarming rate, not just in New York but across the country, far fewer tenants were seeking office space than had been hoped for. The Empire State Building opened with an occupancy rate of only 23 percent—less than half of what would have been expected during normal times. It was a rough start. By the end of the year, many would take to calling Smith's masterwork "The Empty State Building."

One bright spot was the observation decks. By charging a dollar for adults and 25 cents for children, it was not long before the decks were bringing in $3,100 a day. In the building's first year, observatories on the eighty-sixth and one hundred and first floors took in over $800,000 in ticket and trinket sales.

Unfortunately, though, given the Empire State Building's notoriety and height, its observation decks soon became a target for "leapers," those bent on killing themselves with a dramatic lunge from great heights. The first successful suicide from the eighty-sixth floor took place in February 1935. According to Tauranac:

> Irma Eberhardt had thought her boyfriend was seeing other women and was not paying enough attention to her. . . . She asked a guide questions and seemed interested in his answers, but she nodded absentmindedly. The guard turned away to tend to other business, and the next thing he knew she was "atop

Although the Empire State Building initially had trouble filling its commercial space, the observation deck *(above)* at the top of the structure became a reliable source of income. Visitors paid a small fee to enjoy panoramic views of the city. On a clear day, they could see as far as 80 miles out.

the parapet, swaying in the howling wind, and leaped, sailing out into space like a huge bird. The wind was howling, and she cleared the 48-foot horizontal ledge two stories below her."

Though the management of the Empire State Building made every effort to prevent suicides by stationing psychologically trained guards, and, eventually, erecting an inward-curving metal-spike barrier, Irma Eberhardt's successful leap would not

---

EMPIRE STATE BUILDING FACTS:
Emphasis on the Peculiar

The basic facts about the Empire State Building—what it consists of and how long it took to build—are well known. Following are some less-well-known bits and pieces, compiled by the *New York Times* in April 2006:

★ Eight hundred and fifty tenants are listed on the lobby directory.
★ An estimated 9,000 workers show up every day.
★ The most expensive office space, on the seventy-sixth floor, rents for $55 a square foot.
★ The least expensive space, storage on the sixth floor, goes for just $7.40 a square foot.

In the April 23, 2006, edition of the *Times*, Jeff VanDam addressed a few simple questions and curiosities:

★ Why is there is no water tank atop the Empire State Building? The contractors were ahead of their time. The building has a pump system, with water tanks stationed every 20 floors.
★ What is the building's daily trash output? It amounts to 3.23 tons, or the curb weight of a 2006 Hummer H2.
★ What would happen to that fabled penny if it were dropped from the Empire State Building? When wind hits the building,

be the last. In the next dozen years, nine more people jumped to their deaths from the eighty-sixth-floor observation deck.

WAR BEACON

Despite Smith's attempts to attract tenants (primarily through endless publicity gimmicks and the hiring of the public relations firm Publicity Associates), as the Depression worsened, so did prospects for the Empire State Building. The former governor

it travels up the side and creates an updraft. As a result, anything like a penny is likely to be blown back.

Geraldine B. Wagner, in her wonderful book *Thirteen Months To Go: The Creation of the Empire State Building*, has come up with some truly unusual building facts, a few of which are as follows:

★ There is enough floor space to shelter 80,000 people.
★ The building requires 250 cleaners to keep it in shape.
★ More than 200 species of insects have been sucked up by strong winds and collected on the Empire State Building.
★ Minneapolis Honeywell installed a gyroscope on the building and found that, in a high wind, the Empire State Building shifts no more than ¼ inch off center, with a total sway of ½ inch.
★ You can get an electric thrill on top of the Empire State Building if you are wearing rubber-soled shoes.
★ The tower had been struck by lightning 500 times by the 1950s—19 times in one storm alone. The tower acts like a lightning rod, shielding other buildings within a ¼-mile radius.

was soon forced to beg—he pleaded with state agencies to take up residency in his building. In a speech to his successor, Governor Franklin Roosevelt, Smith declared (as reported by Tauranac), "This building is named after the Empire State of our Union. . . . The State of New York can use this building any time it wants to. The governor can have a meeting up here, and if the session lasts into the warm weather he can bring the thirty-day bills up on the roof here and we will provide him with lemonade, and he can dispose of the state's business at the highest point on the continent." The state said thanks, but no thanks.

By 1936, much of the Empire State Building was, indeed, the Empty State Building. There was no elevator service from the forty-fifth to the eightieth floor. With only two exceptions, the building was completely empty of tenants from the forty-first floor up. The upper floors were bare, without partitions, unfinished, and untenanted. At night, however, one would never guess the void that prevailed in the upper half of the Empire State Building. Management decided to keep lights burning on the upper floors, to prevent the tower from looking as if it was floating.

For all the goofy publicity that Smith and his associates sought, they did score big—really big—in 1933, with the release of the movie *King Kong*. The film featured a giant ape that, after rampaging through New York, drags a beautiful blonde, played by actress Fay Wray, to the pinnacle atop the mooring tower. One could not buy such publicity at any price. Visits to the top soared following the movie's debut, contributing vital income that kept the Empire State Building from outright bankruptcy.

Though the Empire State Building struggled through the dark years of the 1930s Depression, the advent of America's involvement in World War II finally drove it toward financial solvency (as it did for many other American enterprises). In January 1942, the regional bureau of the Office of Price Administration leased five full floors of office space—a total of 80,000 square feet. It

The Empire State Building was featured in the 1933 film classic *King Kong*. The movie's main character, a giant ape, swatted at army airplanes while standing on top of the building *(above)*. The film's popularity caused a surge in visits to the observation deck.

was a harbinger of good things to come. Later that year, Schenley Liquor also took five floors and filled them with 800 employees. At last, the Empire State Building was filling up.

Situated as it was in midtown Manhattan, with a reach to the sky like no other structure, the Empire State Building was in a unique position to play a vital role in national defense. "In 1941, when Pearl Harbor was attacked, bringing the United States into World War II, the top of the Empire State Building was used for antiaircraft surveillance," Wagner noted. "Stairwells and fire stairs in the middle of the building became air raid shelters. All windows and the tower were blacked out."

Spotters were all volunteers—at first World War I veterans, mainly American Legionnaires. "But as the war progressed, a broader cross section of volunteers came to man the outposts twenty-four hours a day in shifts as long as eight hours," Tauranac reported. "When a plane was spotted, its description and course was immediately called in to Army Interceptor Command."

If an air raid should actually occur, an event by no means dismissed as far-fetched, plans called for immediate action. Tenants and visitors above the eightieth floor would be taken by elevator to landings between the eighteenth and thirty-second floors. From then on, nobody would be allowed to use the elevators. Everyone would stay put.

By war's end, the Empire State Building had proven itself a good patriot. "Once regarded primarily as a tourist attraction, it was now hailed for having played a major role in aiding the national defense of the country," Berman declared. "The building had supported the patriotic war effort."

It would seem, too, that as the war was about to be won in the summer of 1945, the Empire State Building had escaped unscathed in its efforts to keep the country secure. Then, on July 28, 1945, a few weeks before the Japanese surrender that ended World War II, disaster struck. An Army Air Corps B-25 bomber smashed into the north wall of the Empire State Building.

BOMBER BUST

July 28 was a cool, fog-shrouded day all along the eastern seaboard of the United States. It was a Saturday, a day when some tenants would be at work in the Empire State Building, given the press of war-related activities; however, most fortunately, the number would not be anywhere near the full complement of 15,000 workers the building serviced Monday through Friday. As the fog descended, airports in the region prepared to "go below weather minimums" for landings and takeoffs. It was not a day to fly if one could avoid it. Colonel William Franklin Smith, Jr., preparing for a flight from the Bedford Army Airfield in Bedford, Massachusetts, to Newark, New Jersey, should have grounded himself. July 28 would be the young pilot's last day on Earth.

Smith was an experienced flyer, having only recently returned from the European theater after completing 50 combat missions over Germany and France. Yet he had been flying B-17 bombers, not the unarmed, 12-ton B-25 he now piloted. Smith had flown a B-25 only once before.

As the pilot took off from Bedford with two passengers aboard, he headed south for his destination at the Newark airfield. Having been denied a request to fly to Newark because of poor visibility at the New Jersey airport, Smith took off illegally for New York City's La Guardia Airport, 15 miles northeast of his intended destination. It appears that Smith, once in the New York-New Jersey area, hoped to make a beeline for Newark, bypassing La Guardia altogether.

On the flight south, Smith kept having to fly lower and lower; visibility diminished every minute. By 15 miles north of La Guardia Field, at 9:45 A.M., the pilot was cruising at 250 miles per hour and only 650 feet above ground.

Flying visually (contact) with no instruments, at 9:52 A.M. Smith's *Feather Merchant* B-25 Mitchell turned southwest and descended to a mere 500 feet as he entered New York's airspace. His rendezvous with destiny was at hand.

"At the Triborough Bridge, Smith turned east, obviously confusing the East River with the Hudson River," Michael Lemish recounted in *Aviation* magazine. "With limited visibility because of the fog, Welfare Island probably seemed like part of Manhattan. Smith lowered the landing gear and prepared for what he thought was the final approach. The error quickly manifested itself as the B-25 hurtled just above Manhattan at close to 400 feet per second."

In a matter of moments, Smith banked sharply to avoid the RCA Building and Rockefeller Center. He now flew south, parallel to Fifth Avenue. Stan Lomax, a radio sports announcer for

BUILDING AMERICA NOW

HEARST TOWER

Location New York
Architect Foster & Partners
Height 597 ft.
Materials Steel and Glass
Completion Date 2006

The Hearst Tower, built atop the original six-story Hearst Building in midtown Manhattan, is possibly the most "green," environmentally friendly skyscraper ever built. On September 22, 2006, the 856,000-square-foot office tower was the first building in New York City to receive the Gold Leadership in Energy and Environmental Design (LEED) certificate. Built using an innovative *diagrid* (a contraction of "diagonal grid"), the structure creates a series of four-story triangles on the facade. No vertical steel beams are used. As a result, it is estimated that nearly 2,000 tons of steel were saved in its construction, a 20 percent reduction from a typical office building.

A particularly innovative environmental technology involves the collection and recycling of rainwater on the building's roof. According to the Hearst Tower Web site (http://www.hearstcorp.com/tower/), "The rainwater will be used to replace water lost to evaporation in the office air-conditioning system. It also will be fed into a special pumping system to irrigate plantings and trees inside and outside the building. It is expected that the captured rain will produce about half of the watering needs."

WOR, looked up to see the underside of the B-25 and shouted, on the air, "Climb, you damn fool, climb!" It was too late. Lemish described the final moments:

> At 975 feet above ground, with the nose pitched skyward and the engines screaming, the cockpit of the 12-ton airplane hit the 79th floor of the Empire State Building and the offices of the Catholic War Relief Services. Three people sitting at their desks were crushed instantly, along with the airplane's occupants.

STRUCTURAL INTEGRITY

Upon impact, the airplane's wings sheared clean off. Most of the fuselage tore through the building. One engine and the landing gear flew through internal office walls, across a stairway, and out the south wall of the building. Some parts landed as far away as 10 West 33rd Street. An 18-by-20-foot gash had been taken out of the Empire State Building.

When the bomber hit, its fuel tanks exploded and sent flames racing across the seventy-ninth floor. According to eyewitnesses, everything shook, which caused the 365,000-ton building to sway 2 feet as a result of the force of the impact and the subsequent explosion.

In all, 14 people were killed by the crash—3 in the bomber and 11 in the building (25 more were seriously injured). "Those who were on the direct line with the crash were either killed outright by the impact or by the explosion, mummified in the positions they had assumed when the crash occurred," Tauranac wrote. "Several who were running from the flames were overtaken by them and engulfed. Of the eleven who were killed from the office staff, only one was recognizable, and he had been thrown from his office and had landed on the setback of the seventy-second floor."

Most of the bodies were burned beyond the point at which one could distinguish between male and female. In one case, the heat from the fire had seared a woman's blouse onto her chest. One woman, however, was lucky. Betty Lou Oliver, an elevator operator on the last day of her summer job, was blown out of her post on the eightieth floor when the bomber hit the building. She was badly burned. Rescue workers quickly put Oliver into an adjacent elevator and sent her down to a waiting ambulance. According to William Roberts in *Elevator World*, "As the elevator doors closed, rescue workers heard what sounded like a gunshot but what was, in fact, the snapping of elevator cables weakened by the crash. The car with Oliver inside, now at the 75th floor, plunged to the sub-basement, a fall of over 1,000 feet. Rescuers had to cut a hole in the car to get to the badly injured elevator operator."

How was it that Oliver could have survived such a descent? The elevator car safety device could not set because the governor cable had snapped. Yet Roberts is quick to explain how two factors contributed to slowing the elevator and "cushioning" its fall:

> As the elevator fell, the compensating cables, hanging from beneath the car, piled up in the pit and acted as a coiled spring, slowing the elevator. Also, the hatchway was of a "high-pressure" design, with minimum clearance around the car. In such a small space, the air was compressed under the falling elevator. With such a tight fit of the car in the hatchway, the trapped air created an air cushion in the lower portion of the shaft—thereby further slowing the elevator car and allowing its occupant to survive.

The cost to repair the Empire State Building came to $500,000. Though the restoration took three months, the building was open for business the Monday after the crash. The Empire State Building had been designed with redundancy. There was no progressive collapse, and the building survived. The Empire

In 1945, a B-25 airplane smashed into the seventy-ninth floor of the Empire State Building, killing 14 people. The pilot, trying to fly through the fog, mistakenly directed his airplane toward midtown Manhattan instead of Newark, New Jersey. *Above*, the plane's entry point at the seventy-ninth floor.

State Building's structural integrity had, though in a tragic way, been amply demonstrated.

DESTINATION: EMPIRE STATE BUILDING

In 1944, the year before the bomber crash, the Empire State Building had reached an 85 percent occupancy rate. By 1946, it was fully tenanted. As the second half of the twentieth century took hold, in 1950, *Time* magazine reported that the Empire State Building "was jammed to the rafters." The building was grossing $10 million a year and netting half that sum. Business was thriving, as was tourism. The Empire State Building had become, as *Time* opined, one of the world's most profitable buildings. It was about time.

Observation deck tours attracted the famous, many of whom sought to enhance their celebrity status atop the even more famous building. It is hard to know whether honored flyer Amelia Earhart's trip up, on May 15, 1931, was real or simply planned to garner attention. The following day, the *New York Times* headline proclaimed, "FLIER'S EYES TESTED ATOP EMPIRE STATE: STATUE OF LIBERTY, 4 MILES OFF, IS SUBSTITUTED FOR USUAL JUMBLED ALPHABET." Earhart and other pilots visited the eighty-sixth floor observation deck to engage in, as the *Times* reported, "occupational analysis whereby glasses are prescribed on the basis of the work that the eyes are required to do with them." Earhart, it seems—after staring out at the Statue of Liberty—rated 98 percent in general eyesight efficiency.

Notables continued to visit what was now, in the 1950s, recognized as the most famous building in the world. In October 1957, Queen Elizabeth II of England stood atop the eighty-sixth floor and, commenting on the view, declared, "It is the most beautiful thing I have ever seen." Later in the day, her Majesty was presented with a gold-plated model of the building from Tiffany & Co.

The 1950s would turn out to be, according to Maria Elena Velardi, author of *The Empire State Building and Manhattan Skyscrapers*, the golden era of the Empire State Building. In 1956, the first of what would be many spectacular attempts to light the building took place. In that year, the "Freedom Lights" were installed as part of "Operation: Light Up the Sky"; they were declared to be, at seven feet in diameter, the world's most powerful beacons. "The idea was to have the Empire State Building compete with the Statue of Liberty as the monument welcoming immigrants and visitors to the land of opportunity as more and more were arriving by air than by sea," Velardi declared. "During these years the Empire State Building became not only one of the world's most successful real estate operations, but also the most prestigious symbol of this great metropolis."

"SIX VISUAL STATIONS ON THE NEW YORK AIR," blared the *New York Times* headline of July 19, 1931, less than three months after the Empire State Building opened for business. The *Times* continued, "The research experts and experimenters must work rapidly within the next twelve months if the television predictions of leaders in the radio industry are to come true in 1932. So television plans to climb above the sidewalks of New York in hopes that dreams will come true. Images are to leap into space from an aerial atop the mooring mast 1,250 feet up on the Empire State Building."

Another 20 years would pass, however, before the tallest building in the world would contribute its peak to the television revolution. When it did, with a 60-ton, 220-foot-high TV antenna in 1950, the Empire State Building's height shot up to an incredible 1,469.8 feet. For the building owners, the new television antenna that broadcast signals from all of the TV stations in the New York area brought in a sizable annual income of $500,000.

In 1961, the Empire State Associates purchased the Empire State Building for $65 million. Major banking and brokerage firms, such as Manufacturer's Hanover and Irving Trust, filled the office space. It would seem that, even if the building could not reach higher physically, its value would continue to soar. This is not, however, the way it would turn out.

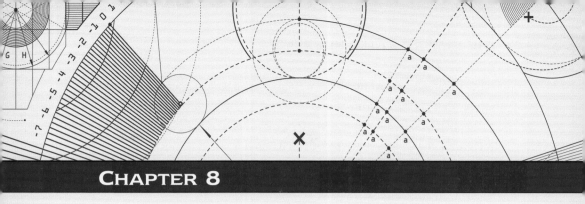

CHAPTER 8

New York's Exclamation Point!

By midcentury, when the Empire State Building was fully rented, its value had risen to match its height. Perhaps now was the time to sell? Perhaps it was time for Raskob and associates to cash out what had become one of the world's most profitable buildings?

In May 1951, the Realty Associates Securities Corporation, led by Roger L. Stevens, made a $50 million offer for the 20-year-old Empire State Building. The bid was quickly accepted. However, the closing (signing) of possibly the most complex real estate deal in history would not be accomplished with the simple swipe of a pen across a few forms. As described by Tauranac, there was a lot more to it than that:

> The closing took place in December 1951, in the boardroom of the Bankers Trust Company offices at 16 Wall Street. It had been preceded by an all-day rehearsal the day before to check and seal the hundreds of documents required to consummate the transaction. A second closing at the Empire State Building

that had all the hallmarks of a Hollywood first night was staged for the benefit of the press. The checks were already safely deposited in vaults in the Wall Street offices of Bankers Trust, but for the public record Stevens handed a token check to representatives of Raskob's heirs. Flashbulbs popped, television

THE WORLD'S TALLEST SKYSCRAPERS

A skyscraper is a building that is at least 20 stories high. Some skyscraper buffs insist that, when calculating building height, it is okay to go beyond stories or floors and count flagpoles, antennas, and spires. Others think that just habitable space—residential or office—should be considered. To the latter, observation towers, communication towers, and the like are structures—not buildings.

Sticking to the more conservative definition, in which television towers and masts are not part of the height calculation, the list of the world's tallest buildings (as of the fall of 2007) is as follows:

#	BUILDING	CITY	HEIGHT (M)	HEIGHT (FT)	FLOORS	YEAR
1.	Taipei 101	Taipei	509	1,671	101	2004
2.	Petronas Tower 1	Kuala Lumpur	452	1,483	88	1998
3.	Petronas Tower 2	Kuala Lumpur	452	1,483	88	1998
4.	Sears Tower	Chicago	442	1,451	108	1974
5.	Jin Mao Tower	Shanghai	421	1,380	88	1999
6.	Two Int. Finance	Hong Kong	415	1,362	88	2003
7.	CITIC Plaza	Guangzhou	391	1,283	80	1997

cameras whirred, and the principals—clutching little models of the building—posed again and again.

In 1954, the Empire State Building was sold a second time, to Colonel Henry Crown, for what seemed like a loss but actually

#	BUILDING	CITY	HEIGHT (M)	HEIGHT (FT)	FLOORS	YEAR
8.	Shun Hing Square	Shenzhen	384	1,260	69	1996
9.	Empire State	New York	381	1,250	102	1931
10.	Central Plaza	Hong Kong	374	1,227	78	1992
11.	Bank of China Tower	Hong Kong	367	1,205	70	1990
12.	Emirates Office	Dubai	355	1,163	54	2000
13.	Tuntex Sky Tower	Kaohsiung	348	1,140	85	1997
14.	Aon Center	Chicago	346	1,136	83	1973
15.	The Center	Hong Kong	346	1,135	73	1998
16.	John Hancock	Chicago	344	1,127	100	1969
17.	Rose Tower	Dubai	333	1,093	72	2007
18.	Shimao Int. Plaza	Shanghai	333	1,093	60	2006
19.	Minsheng Bank	Wuhan	331	1,087	68	2007
20.	Ryugyong Hotel	Pyongyang	330	1,083	105	1992

Source: Emporis Standards Committee (ESC)

was not when operating costs and depreciation were figured in. The price for the second sale was $49.5 million. Crown hung on until the third exchange of owners, which took place in 1961. Now things would get interesting and complicated, with ramifications for decades to come.

Purchased by a syndicate called Empire State Associates (led by Lawrence A. Wien), the $82 million paid ($65 million for the building plus $17 million for the land) was the largest sum ever spent for a building. With the Empire State Building now in hand, so to speak, Wien—in a complex real estate transaction—quickly transferred legal title to Prudential Life Insurance Company. The real estate tycoon then did something extraordinary: He leased back the Empire State Building for a total of 114 years, through January 2076.

Under what would soon come to be known as the Master Lease, the lessee (Empire State Associates) would pay Prudential a paltry average annual sum of $2.2 million for control of 2.5 million square feet of the most desirable building in the world. Prudential, of course, felt that it was getting a good deal—in 1960s dollars, perhaps they were. Yet, soon enough, Wien and his associates were raking in a cool $10.5 million annually by subleasing to hundreds of building tenants. During the ensuing decades, the "lease of a lifetime" (literally) would look better and better. It was not who owned the Empire State Building (Prudential) that mattered; it was who owned the Master Lease (Empire State Associates).

With the property at Fifth Avenue and 34th Street now encumbered with a Master Lease that required the lessee to pay whomever owned the building an average annual income of $2.2 million, the building itself was actually worth a lot less than it would seem. In the late 1990s, the Empire State Building again went on the block, but for what would strike anyone as a ridiculously low price of $60 million. Unburdened by the Master Lease (under which a purchaser could rent directly to tenants), some estimated that the Empire State Building, at the turn of the twenty-first century, was worth close to a billion dollars.

TWIN TOWERS CHALLENGE

It took 40 years to happen, but—when completed in 1972—the first of two World Trade Center towers surpassed the Empire State Building in height. The North Tower, which had 110 stories, stood an astonishing 1,368 feet above ground. Its twin, the South Tower, which was completed a year later, topped out its 110 stories at 1,362 feet. The art deco Empire State Building,

Completed in 1972, the World Trade Center's Twin Towers *(above)* became the tallest structures in the world, surpassing the Empire State Building's height by more than 100 feet. Designed as tube buildings, the Twin Towers were able to support over 100 floors and withstand heavy winds.

two-and-half miles uptown, now had to settle for third place in the new height upmanship gripping New York and the nation.

Not all New Yorkers welcomed the Twin Towers to the city's skyline. Many saw the 87-by-135-feet rectangular monoliths as nothing more than "giant shoeboxes." Their office windows were only 18 inches wide, thus impairing the view from the two buildings. Supposedly, this design element reflected architect Minoru Yamasaki's fear of heights. He felt that the narrow windows added to a sense of security for the occupants.

Aesthetic criticisms notwithstanding, the Twin Towers reflected major innovations in skyscraper structural design. Conceived as framed tube structures, the Twin Towers were constructed around a central core of 47 interior columns. The cores, which acted as the spine of the buildings, housed the elevator shafts, utility shafts, restrooms, and stairwells; they supported the gravity loads of their towers.

Surrounding the core were 59 perimeter columns along each building facade. These columns supported the lateral (wind) loads of the Twin Towers. In doing this, the architect moved the building's steel to the outside, where it was needed most. As a result, the buildings were both light and rigid. They had, as Rasenberger framed it, "the spine of a vertebrate and the shell of a crustacean."

Even before completion of the first Twin Tower, an Empire State Building response was readied, though it may have been only a "floater" to gauge public reaction. "The owners of the 102-story Empire State Building, the Colossus of the skies for almost 40 years and about to be relegated to the indignity of third place among the world's highest buildings, are exploring the possibilities of adding 11 stories and making the building once again the world's tallest," reported the *New York Times* on October 11, 1972.

New Yorkers, and the world, were stunned. Was there no end to the race to be number one? As the *Times* continued, "According to tentative sketches drawn up by Shreve, Lamb, and Harmon, the original architects for the building, the 16-story tower [mooring mast] on top of the building would be torn down and the six stories beneath that would be remodeled and encompassed within a new 33-story structure, probably with an exterior of glass and a restaurant at the top."

The plan to stretch the Empire State Building caused problems, however—problems beyond the indignity of such a jarring "remodeling" of the American icon. How to increase elevator space to accommodate an additional 33 floors was just the beginning of the challenges the architects and designers would face. Plumbing for the entire building would have to be reworked. There also was the "slight" problem of how to demolish 16 floors more than 1,000 feet above ground. The conceiver of the plan, Robert W. Jones, responded to the last issue by declaring, as quoted in the *Times*, "If you can get it up there, you can get it down. Each man kills the thing he loves."

Love, at least for the idea of extending the Empire State Building in such a violent manner, was in short supply. Management soon disavowed Jones's plan, claiming they never seriously contemplated adding anything to the Empire State Building. They would, it seems, have to reconcile themselves to the fact that, even if their 1930s structure was no longer the world's tallest, it was at least the "world's most famous."

CONCRETE'S THREAT

"They don't build them like they used to" is a phrase that suggests things were done better in the old days than they are now. Whether or not this is true, skyscrapers in the last few decades, since the rise of the World Trade Center Twin Towers, are not what they were in the time of the Chrysler Building, the Manhattan Building, and the Empire State Building. True, the basic design concept of a supporting cage frame with curtain walls to provide protection from the elements (skeleton and skin) has not changed in the last 100 years. Yet, as anyone can see by glancing upward, today's skyscraper walls have become thinner and thinner—often as thin as glass, which is what many of them are. Even more significant, though, is what has changed under the skin. More and more, ironworkers no longer ply their steel-framing trade. Concrete, not steel, has become the architect's preferred choice for structural support. Columns, girders, and beams are increasingly made of the reinforced mix.

Concrete (a mixture of cement, sand, gravel, and water) is, by itself, capable of withstanding tremendous compression loads but not much tension or torsion. "If you hold a pencil in a vertical position with the point on a table or desk and push on the top of the pencil, you will be creating a compression load," explains Alfred Morgan in *The Story of Skyscrapers*. "If you grasp the pencil in both hands and twist it, the load upon the pencil will be a torsion strain. The blade of a screwdriver is subject to a torsion strain when you drive a screw. Trying to pull the pencil apart from opposite ends is a tensile strain."

Reinforced concrete is concrete with steel reinforcing bars set in place as the concrete mixture is poured into wooden forms. Like fibers in a stalk of celery, concrete that is reinforced is tremendously strong.

Concrete has many advantages over steel in the construction of high-rise buildings, perhaps the most significant being the lower distance created between floors. Concrete slabs, even after wiring and ceiling fixtures are added to the bottom and floorboards and carpet to the top, are 8 or 9 inches thick. Using steel framing, the comparable distance is 15 inches. A savings of 6 inches per floor may not seem like much; however, as Rasenberger explains, "Multiplied by 70 stories, this comes out to about 40 feet. That's 40 fewer feet of facade to cover the perimeter of the building; 40 fewer feet of wires and pipes running inside the building; 40 fewer feet to brace against wind pressure; several million fewer dollars spent on construction."

Steel is far from dead—far from being relegated to bridge work and oil tanker hulls. Although steel buildings are harder to construct, they are far more malleable when completed. In other words, steel structures can be renovated more easily. "Bashing a hole through a floor or trying to move a column is an expensive and elaborate procedure in a concrete building but is easily achieved in a steel building," Rasenberger noted. "Also, steel is better suited to longer spans, the kind of long spans you are likely to encounter in office building lobbies and television studios."

Steel or concrete—or, in many cases, a combination of both—skyscrapers have climbed ever higher in the last few years. Higher, that is, when they are not crashing down to the ground.

TALLEST ONCE MORE

On the morning of September 11, 2001, two commandeered Boeing jetliners, each traveling at 500 miles per hour and filled with 10,000 gallons of jet fuel, slammed into first one and then the other of the Word Trade Center's Twin Towers. It is doubtful there existed, anywhere, a structure that could have remained standing after taking such a hit. Yet the Twin Towers stood—at least for a while. "The structural damage sustained by each of the two buildings as a result of the terrorist attacks was massive," a federal study reported, as quoted in *High Steel: The Daring Men Who Built the World's Greatest Skyline*. "The fact that the structures were able to sustain the level of damage and remain standing for an extended period of time is remarkable and the reason that most building occupants were able to evacuate safely."

Yet the two Towers did come down; the intense heat fueled by the spreading gasoline caused their eventual collapse. Structural steel loses about half its strength at 1,200 degrees Fahrenheit, and the World Trade Center fires reached an estimated 1,300 to 1,400 degrees Fahrenheit. The fires from the planes, which covered an entire floor almost instantly, weakened each tower's support structure. Weakened floors began to collapse and crash into the floors below. The weight of the plunging floors accelerated, and the exterior walls buckled. In a matter of minutes, a 110-floor structure became a pile of rubble only a few stories high.

In the days and weeks following 9/11, ironworkers were called in to clean up the mess at Ground Zero in a reverse of their traditional construction roles. "What distinguished the ironworkers from the masses who responded to the disaster in those early days was the skill they possessed," reported Rasenberger. "It was like Mickey [an ironworker] said: *There was nobody more equipped to do it.* The most important project of those early days—and indeed for months to come—was the careful but steady removal of structural steel. Cutting steel. Rigging steel. Hoisting steel. *This is what we do every day.*"

With the collapse of the Twin Towers, the Empire State Building became, once more, New York's tallest building. Yet, in the last decades of the twentieth century—when the iconic colossus remained in the shadow of the Twin Towers—the Empire State Building, some would insist, had begun to lose its shine. It had become, they said, a tarnished gem.

In 1983, to celebrate the fiftieth anniversary of the original King Kong movie, an 80-foot, air-filled replica of the ape was tied to the mooring mast as part of a publicity stunt. Gusts of wind soon tore the replica apart, and it quickly deflated. Some thought the whole affair was just a tacky reflection of the Empire State Building's new status. "There has always been a gulf between the public perception of the Empire State Building and the reality of the building as a workaday office building," Pacelle noted in *Empire: A Tale of Obsession, Betrayal, and the Battle for an American Icon.* "By the mid-1990s, the disconnect was wide."

It did not help, of course, that a purposeful trashing of the building's image was being carried out by a publicity-seeking real estate mogul named Donald Trump. In an attempt to acquire partial ownership of the Empire State Building in the 1990s, "The Donald" was on a campaign to discredit the owners of the Master Lease, Malkin and Helmsley, by suggesting they were not keeping the Empire State Building in good condition (a violation of the lease agreement). Trump claimed that the building was no longer "high class." He told reporters that the Empire State Building was a mess, "a laughing stock." "It displayed," he claimed, "a lack of quality throughout."

BUILDING AMERICA NOW

NEW YORK TIMES BUILDING

Location New York
Architect Renzo Piano and Fox & Fowle
Height 748 ft.
Materials Steel and Glass
Completion Date 2007

The New York Times Building, located in Times Square, is said to be the most significant new building designed for the New York City skyline in decades. With a height of 1,046 feet (including antenna and spire), the building—which was completed in the fall of 2007—is currently tied with the Chrysler Building for the second-tallest building in the city. The New York Times Building, which includes 52 floors and 1.54 million square feet of rentable office space, is expected to revitalize the Times Square area, which was named after the *New York Times* in 1904.

An innovative feature of the building is its use of thousands of small ceramic tubes that contain ultra-clear low-iron glass and are draped horizontally in front of the glass curtain wall, designed to reduce the building's cooling loads. The tubes, which act as a sunscreen, reflect light and change colors throughout the day. Furthering its environmentally friendly nature, the New York Times Building contains mechanized shades that work in concert with more than 20,000 dimmable fluorescent fixtures to maintain needed light levels while saving energy and preventing glare.

By the mid-1990s, the Empire State Building saw its occupancy level slide from 91 percent to 82 percent. Bad publicity, fueled by Trump's criticisms, clearly had adverse effects.

AMERICA'S EXCLAMATION POINT!

Such negative events took a deadly turn when, on February 23, 1997, a 69-year-old Palestinian named Ali Abu Kamal made a visit to the Empire State Building's eighty-sixth floor observation deck, where he joined about 100 happy sightseers on the outdoor promenade. "I love Americans and I love America," he said to no one in particular, as reported by Pacelle.

"'Where are you from?' someone asked."

"'I'm from Egypt,' he responded."

Abu Kamal then walked to the southeast corner of the outdoor deck, drew out a .380-caliber black Beretta, and began firing as he walked along the deck. Within less than a minute, eight people were shot, six fatally. A moment later, Abu Kamal pressed the gun to his head and pulled the trigger.

Security, it was later determined, was clearly deficient at the Empire State Building. From then on, all bags and packages would be inspected and armed guards would be posted on the eighty-sixth floor.

Yet, as with so many events in the Empire State Building's history, by the time it turned 75 years old (in 2006), good seemed to triumph over evil. An astonishing 3.5 million visitors a year—12,000 a day—made it to the top to look out from the same observation deck where Abu Kamal had gone on his murderous rampage nearly a decade earlier. The current owners, Wien & Malkin, have committed to an astonishing $550 million makeover that, according to Amy Cortese of the *New York Times*, "will modernize the building's infrastructure, including elevators, the air-conditioning system and the rest of the rooms, and convert its rabbit-warren floors into gleaming new spaces."

Still, there is room for criticism. As is usual in such cases, such censure often comes from those who love the object of

Hovering over the New York skyline, the Empire State Building has once again become the city's tallest building. Over 75 years old, the structure is colorfully lit every night and remains a symbol of the city's exuberant spirit.

their disapproval the most. One such person is Ronnette Riley, an architect with offices on the seventy-fourth floor of the Empire State Building.

Established in 1987, Ronnette Riley Architect (RRA) provides services mostly in the modernist vocabulary. One of the few women running an architecture firm in America today, Ms. Riley is not afraid of heights. With spacious offices on the seventy-fourth floor, she may be the highest residing architect in the land.

Having worked in the Empire State Building since her firm's conception, Riley has seen her beloved building take turns she has not always liked. "They want to carpet the halls," she told the author during his 2007 visit to her stylish offices. "They have already put vinyl wall covering over the marble walls in the elevator lobbies. They are tearing out the wonderful old metal doors and transoms and putting short solid wood doors in their place. They have renovated the beautiful black and white bathrooms to now look like the very worst 1970s low rent office-building beige, brown, and pink bathrooms.

"They just don't get it" is Ms. Riley's main concern. "They don't understand that the building's very appeal remains its art deco design and construction."

Riley should know. The architect has what may well be the largest private collection of Empire State Building memorabilia in existence. In addition to countless photographs, postcards, and documents, her office displays well over 100 souvenir models of the building she truly loves. Her favorite is an animal squeeze toy of the Empire State Building. Purple and fat, it is designed to withstand the toothy attacks of a ravaging dog.

The building itself is made to last as well. On its seventy-fifth anniversary, the Empire State Building remained largely undiminished in the public eye. "Unique among office buildings," declared Pacelle, "it lives on as a monument, a sturdy lighthouse on the New York skyline for generations of travelers dropping down out of the clouds after a long-distance flight or cresting New Jersey's palisades on the way home."

In 2031, when the Empire State Building celebrates its one-hundredth birthday, it will have long since relinquished its title as the tallest building in New York. It will, however, most assuredly remain the city's, the nation's, and perhaps the world's most illustrious office structure ever.

1897	Waldorf-Astoria Hotel is completed and opens for business.
1916	New York City passes the nation's first zoning law that mandates setbacks for skyscrapers.
1929	*September* Starrett Brothers & Eken are hired to construct Empire State Building.
	October Waldorf-Astoria Hotel demolition begins.
	October 29 Stock market crashes, ushering in the Great Depression.
1930	*March* Demolition of Waldorf-Astoria is completed; excavation of Empire State Building begins.

TIMELINE

1929
September Starrett Brothers & Eken are hired to construct Empire State Building.

1916
New York City passes the nation's first zoning law that mandates set-backs for skyscrapers.

1916 ———— **1930**

1930

March Demolition of Waldorf-Astoria is completed; excavation of Empire State Building begins.

September Structural steel frame of Empire State Building is completed.

September Structural steel frame of Empire State Building is completed.

November Exterior stone work on Empire State Building is completed.

1931 *May 1* Empire State Building officially opens.

1933 *King Kong* movie provides great publicity for Empire State Building.

1941–1945 During World War II, occupancy rate soars.

1945 *July* B-25 bomber crashes into Empire State Building, killing 14 people.

1956 "Freedom Lights" are placed atop Empire State Building.

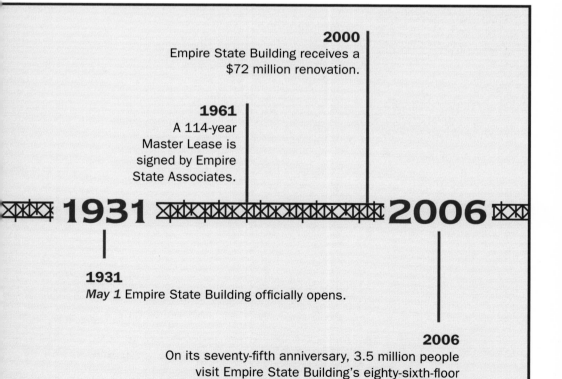

2000
Empire State Building receives a
$72 million renovation.

1961
A 114-year
Master Lease is
signed by Empire
State Associates.

1931 2006

1931
May 1 Empire State Building officially opens.

2006
On its seventy-fifth anniversary, 3.5 million people
visit Empire State Building's eighty-sixth-floor
observation deck.

1961	A 114-year Master Lease is signed by Empire State Associates.
1972	Twin Towers are completed, erasing Empire State Building's status as the tallest building in the world.
2000	Empire State Building receives a $72 million renovation.
2001	*September 11* The World Trade Center is destroyed; Empire State Building is once again the tallest structure in New York City.
2006	On its seventy-fifth anniversary, 3.5 million people visit Empire State Building's eighty-sixth-floor observation deck.

acrophobic   Abnormal dread of high places.

Art deco   A popular design style of the 1920s and 1930s that emphasized bold outlines, geometric and zigzag forms, and the use of metal and plastic.

beam   A rigid structural member designed to carry loads across space to supporting elements, usually columns.

bedrock   An unbroken, solid rock that underlies soil, clay, sand, or rock fragments.

campanile   A freestanding bell tower.

cantilever   A projecting beam or member supported at only one end.

cement   A mixture of clay and limestone, finely pulverized and used as an ingredient in concrete and mortar.

column   A rigid, relatively slender, vertical pillar designed to support compression loads.

concrete   A stonelike building material made by mixing cement and various mineral aggregates with water to cause the cement to set and bind the entire mass.

curtain wall   An exterior wall supported entirely by the structural frame of a building and carrying no loads other than its own weight and wind loads.

cupola   A small structure built on top of a roof.

dirigible   A lighter-than-air airship capable of being steered.

edifice   A large, massive structure.

filigree   Ornamental work.

flapper   A young woman of the 1920s who showed a great deal of freedom from convention.

foundation   The lowest division of a building, partly or wholly below the surface of the ground. The foundation is designed to support and anchor the superstructure and transmit its loads directly to Earth.

frame   A skeletal structure of relatively slender members designed to give shape and support to a building.

gargoyle   A figure in the form of a grotesque human or animal.

girder   A large principal beam designed to support concentrated loads.

granite   An extremely hard, coarse-grained igneous rock composed mainly of quartz, feldspar, and mica.

grillage   A framework of crossing beams for spreading heavy loads over large areas.

I-beam   A rolled or extruded metal beam with a cross section that resembles the capital letter I.

limestone   A sedimentary rock formed chiefly by the accumulation of organic remains, such as shells and coral.

load   Any of the forces to which a structure is subjected.

load-bearing wall   A wall that is capable of supporting an imposed load, as from a floor or roof of a building.

mullion   A slender vertical member that divides windows.

omnibus   An automotive public vehicle designed to carry a large number of people.

parallelepiped   A 6-faced polyhedron whose faces are parallelograms in pairs of parallel planes.

Peacock Alley   A long hallway of the Waldorf-Astoria through which women would parade, showing off their fine clothes (as a peacock would strut its feathers).

pier   A cast-in-place concrete foundation formed by boring a hole in the ground to a bearing stratum and filling it with concrete.

rivet   A metal pin with a head at one end, used to unite two or more plates.

scow   A large, flat-bottomed boat used chiefly to transport bulk.

spandrel   A panel-like area in a multistory building, between the sill of a window on one level and the head of a window immediately below.

spire   A tall, tapered pyramidal structure atop a building.

terra cotta A hard, fired clay, reddish-brown in color when unglazed, used for architectural facings and ornaments.

terrazzo A mosaic floor composed of marble or other stone chips.

vertex The top; summit.

viaduct A long, elevated roadway.

BIBLIOGRAPHY

BOOKS

Bascomb, Neal. *Higher: A Historic Race to the Sky and the Making of a City*. New York: Random House, 2003.

Berman, John S. *The Empire State Building*. New York: Barnes & Noble, 2003.

Ching, Francis. *A Visual Dictionary of Architecture*. New York: John Wiley & Sons, 1995.

Glancey, Jonathan. *The Story of Architecture*. New York: Dorling Kindersley, 2000.

Hawkes, Nigel. *Structures: The Way Things Are Built*. New York: Macmillan, 1993.

Kelly, Thomas. *Empire Rising*. New York: Farrar, Straus and Giroux, 2005.

Kingwell, Mark. *Nearest Thing to Heaven: The Empire State Building and American Dreams*. New Haven, Conn.: Yale University Press, 2006.

Morgan, Alfred. *The Story of Skyscrapers*. New York: Farrar & Rinehart, 1934.

Okrent, Daniel. *Great Fortune: The Epic of Rockefeller Center*. New York: Penguin Books, 2003.

Pacelle, Mitchell. *Empire: A Tale of Obsession, Betrayal, and the Battle for an American Icon*. New York: John Wiley & Sons, 2001.

Rasenberger, Jim. *High Steel: The Daring Men Who Built the World's Greatest Skyline*. New York: HarperCollins, 2004.

Talese, Gay. *The Bridge*. New York: Walker & Company, 1964.

Tauranac, John. *The Empire State Building: The Making of a Landmark*. New York: St. Martin's Griffin, 1995.

Terranova, Antonino. *Skyscrapers*. New York: Barnes & Noble, 2003.

Wagner, Geraldine B. *Thirteen Months to Go: The Creation of the Empire State Building*. San Diego: Thunder Bay Press, 2003.

Willis, Carol. *Building the Empire State Building.* New York: The Skyscraper Museum, 1998.

NEWSPAPER ARTICLES

"Razing of Waldorf Started By Smith." *New York Times*, October 2, 1929.

"Enlarges Site for 1,000-Foot Building." *New York Times*, November 19, 1929.

"Smith Skyscraper to Have Dirigible Mast Towering Quarter of a Mile Above Fifth Avenue." *New York Times*, December 12, 1929.

"$27,500,000 Loan Filed." *New York Times*, December 25, 1929.

"Smith Skyscraper Has a Novel Design." *New York Times*, January 8, 1930.

"Column to Support 5,000 Tons on Empire State Building." *New York Times*, January 10, 1930.

"Airship Flies About Empire State Mast." *New York Times*, December 17, 1930.

"Empire State Tower, Tallest in World, Is Opened by Hoover." *New York Times*, May 2, 1931.

"Panorama Viewed from 85th Story." *New York Times*, May 2, 1931.

"Rivalry for Height Is Seen as Ended." *New York Times*, May 2, 1931.

"Throngs Inspect Tallest Building." *New York Times*, May 3, 1931.

"Big Sunday Crowd Sees Empire Tower." *New York Times*, May 4, 1931.

"Fliers' Eyes Tested Atop Empire State." *New York Times*, May 16, 1931.

"Empire State Club to Open Quarters." *New York Times*, May 23, 1931.

"Many on City's Peak Look Down on Show." *New York Times*, May 24, 1931.

"Empire State Building Called Tower of Babel; Dr. Machen Says Architecture Lacks Soul." *New York Times*, July 13, 1931.

"Six Visual Stations on the New York Air." *New York Times*, July 19, 1931.

"Empire State Roof Pays $3,100 Daily." *New York Times*, October 11, 1931.

Kaempffert, Waldemar. "Empire State Building Proves an Efficient Conductor—The Biggest Spectroscope." *New York Times*, July 9, 1933.

"Empire State Crash Stirs British Public." *New York Times*, July 30, 1945.

"Amid Oil Boom: A New Moscow Rises. *Los Angeles Times*, July 31, 2007.

FILM

Scheftel, Jeff. *Empire State Building*. Jaffe Productions and Hearst Entertainment Television, 1994.

WEB SITES

Empire State Building: Official Internet Site
www.esbnyc.com/index2.cfm?noflassh=1

Infoplease.com: Empire State Building
www.infoplease.com/ce6/us/A0817281.html

A View on Cities: Empire State Building
www.aviewoncities.com/nyc/empirestate.htm

NYCtourist.com: Empire State Building Photo Tour
www.nyctourist.com/empire1.htm

About.com: The Plane That Crashed Into the Empire State Building
www.history1900s.about.com/od/1940s/a/empirecrash.htm

A View on Cities: Chrysler Building
www.aviewoncities.com/nyc/chrysler.htm

Chicago Landmarks: Early Skyscrapers Tour
www.cityofchicago.org/Landmarks/Tours/Skyscrapers.html

Encyclopedia of Chicago: Skyscrapers
www.encyclopedia.chicagohistory.org/pages/1149.html

The Skyscraper Museum
www.skyscraper.org/home.htm

Infoplease.com: The History of Skyscrapers
www.infoplease.com/spot/skyscraperhistory.html

About.com: Skyscrapers and World's Tallest Building
www.architecture.about.com/od/skyscrapers/skyscrapers_and_
 Worlds_Tallest_Building.htm

Skyscrapers: 19th Century Architecture
www.bc.edu/bc_org/avp/cas/fnart/fa267/19_sky.html

SkyscraperPage
www.skyscraperpage.com

FURTHER RESOURCES

Hopkinson, Deborah, and James. E. Ransome. *Sky Boys: How They Built the Empire State Building.* New York: Schwartz & Wade Books, 2006.

Lusted, Marcia Amidon. *The Empire State Building.* New York: Lucent Books, 2005.

Mann, Elizabeth. *Empire State Building.* New York: Mikaya Press, 2003.

Velardi, Maria Elena. *The Empire State Building.* Florence: Casa Editrice Bonechi, 2002.

WEB SITES

Building Big: Databank: Empire State Building
www.pbs.org/wgbh/buildingbig/wonder/structure/empire_state.html

FactMonster.com: Empire State Building
www.factmonster.com/ce6/us/A0817281.html

SkyscraperPage.com: Empire State Building
www.skyscraperpage.com/cities/?buildingID=23

Building Big: All About Skyscrapers
www.pbs.org/wgbh/buildingbig/skyscraper/index.html

About.com: Why the World Trade Center Twin Towers Fell
http://architecture.about.com/library/weekly/aawtc-collapse.htm

PICTURE CREDITS

INDEX

ABOUT THE AUTHOR

RONALD A. REIS has written 18 books, including *The Dust Bowl*, *The New York Subway System* and young adult biographies of Eugenie Clark, Jonas Salk, Ted Williams, Mickey Mantle, and Lou Gehrig. He is chairperson of the Technology Department at Los Angeles Valley College.